Lost in Wonder

Esther de Waal is one of today's most popular authors writing in the field of spirituality. She lives in Herefordshire, close to the border between England and Wales, having returned to the countryside where she grew up. A sense of place has always been important and, after Cambridge, she became the first research student in the newly founded Department of Local History at Leicester. It was the buildings and the landscape that originally encouraged her to explore the Benedictine, Cistercian and Celtic traditions. Her first interests now are her garden and her increasing number of grandchildren, but she also finds time to write, to take retreats and to travel – feeling a particular connection with South Africa.

Lost in Wonder

*Rediscovering the spiritual
art of attentiveness*

Esther de Waal

LITURGICAL PRESS

© Esther de Waal 2003

First published in 2003 by the Canterbury Press Norwich
St Mary's Works, St Mary's Plain, Norwich, Norfolk NR3 3BH

Published in the United States of America by
Liturgical Press, Collegeville, Minnesota 56321

Library of Congress Cataloging-in-Publication data available

ISBN 978-0-8146-3821-7 (paperback)
ISBN 978-0-8146-2992-5 (hardcover)

The Author has asserted her right under the
Copyright, Designs and Patents Act, 1988, to be
identified as the Author of this Work

Typeset by Rowland Phototypesetting Ltd,
Bury St Edmunds, Suffolk.
Printed in the United States of America.

For Ben, Matthew and Anna

Contents

The Starting Point

To take time to be apart, which I consciously give to myself as something positive, creative, is not a luxury, it is essential. The gift of space for myself seems so simple, and in a way it is; but it is also surprisingly difficult to do without some form of external encouragement. And that is the very simple purpose of this book. I am writing of course for my own self, and addressing my own needs. But my hope is that others will find that it can help them too, if only by suggesting a structure and a sense of direction. It is intended as a form of gentle support, and there is never any idea that it should dictate a right way since that must lie entirely with each individual and with God. I have set it out in the form of a number of days that could very easily be used as a guide to making a retreat at home, and that is definitely one of my intentions. However, it can be used in any way at all, and all the practical suggestions can be rejected so that it can be read as a perfectly ordinary book over any length of time. Its purpose is the same in whatever way it is used: to awake us from drift and drowsiness into a fuller and deeper sense of attentiveness to the world around and to the presence of God in that world.

If we fail to find the time to stand back, to give ourselves a break, a breathing space, we are in danger of failing to be fully alive, or to enjoy that fullness of life for which we were created. The reasons for this will vary. At one end of the scale many people today seem to be busier and living under greater stress than ever before. In contrast, at the other end of the scale are those who have too little to do, whose lives are empty, without any sense of purpose and direction, and for whom the danger lies in drifting into lethargy or worse still into quiet despair. In either case the chances are that in Wordsworth's words we have become 'dull of sight' (or as he originally wrote, 'dull of soul'), that we have allowed our inner eye and our gifts of awareness and attentiveness to become dimmed. We need to hear again Christ's very simple command: 'Come and *see*.' I guess that we all know only too well how easily, and often how imperceptibly, the lens with which we view the world can become dull and lifeless. We need to take time to adjust the focus, to re-focus and ask ourselves if we might not have a distorting lens. Above all, I hope that this book will bring the opportunity to take time to clear and refresh the inner eye with which we see the world; and to think and pray about the balance between looking inward in self-interest and looking outward beyond the self to the world around.

Stress or emptiness? Relentless activity or a void? Although both are equally familiar in today's experience, it seems that it is the subject of stress and pressure which gains most attention in popular writing. It remains a subject of perpetual fascination with the media and it is almost impossible today to pick up a glossy magazine without finding some discussion of the increasing stress in today's world. As the pace of life accelerates, pressure confronts us at so many levels: speedier and speedier communication demanding instant response; the information culture threatening overload; clever advertising insidiously attempting to bully or to seduce us into buying certain brand tags and labels, and the message always that we need to earn more and acquire more. We are surrounded by noise, a constant battering of sound, threats of pollution and natural disaster, international crises at all levels. Even the Church makes demands rather than giving us space and silence, asking us to serve on committees or join groups or give practical support to its many excellent ventures. Each one of us can make our own list of the many ways in which these things are encroaching on our lives. And then the consumer world next offers us the correctives, in the gym and the work-out and the health farm, and a plethora of popular books which give us advice on all the survival techniques for the avoidance of stress, the attainment of calm, the fulfilment of self.

At the other end of the pole are those whose lives are threatened by having too much time. What so many of us dreamt of when career or family life were at their most relentless and demanding, and when the idea of space and solitude seemed like some unattainable ideal, now feels like emptiness or desolation. There is of course a positive and a negative way of being empty, though loneliness often removes the energy necessary to make the choice between being empty and open, or empty and closed up, closed in. Loneliness and loss take many forms: redundancy, bereavement, exile, illness, bankruptcy, betrayal, and there is often the underlying danger of failing to turn outwards because the attraction of falling into the inner void appears so much easier.

Whatever it may be, in any particular situation there is the danger that we are wasting the God-given possibility of living life to the full. I long for fullness of life and it is frightening to think that I might be wasting that most precious of God's gifts, the chance to live fully and freely. Stopping to take time to look at the pattern of my life, and to think and pray about it, will almost inevitably mean that I not only learn more about God but I discover more about myself.

As I change, so must my relationship with God. This is of course true of all relationships and not least my relationship with myself, for I must not forget that I am also my own best and closest friend, and that this is something which also needs nurturing. Unless there is the continual renewing, perhaps even the re-forging, of any relationship there is a very real danger that it will cease to be dynamic. Above all it must never lose the element of mystery – and the recovery of mystery will be one of the most significant themes of what I am trying to explore in this book, just as attention, another of the themes of this book, which is generally applied to the physical world around us, also plays a vital role in keeping relationships alive.

❦

Recent years have seen unprecedented growth in retreat-giving and retreat-going. There are now great numbers of centres as well as monastic communities, which offer an opportunity to spend varying lengths of time, from a day to a week-end or longer, in a quiet place, with or without a guide or director. The accommodation may be a simple hermitage, a caravan, or a simple wooden hut in a wood, for example, or a comfortable room in a well-appointed house. But for many of us a time of retreat away from home remains a luxury, whether for financial or physical reasons, commitments to work or family, or whatever form our own particular personal circumstances might take.

This book is written with such people in mind – though again I want to repeat that I hope that it will prove to be a book in which everyone, Christian or not, will find themselves at home. But I am particularly aware of those who are busy at home or at work, those tied to a sick bed or confined to their rooms, those living alone. To remain within surroundings which are familiar, which perhaps even appear commonplace and uninspiring, and yet simultaneously make them the starting off point from which to explore a deeper reality, both within oneself and in one's surroundings, may not seem as easy as it would be away from home. Yet it is something on which it seems important to embark.

Apart from the fact that I am looking for a time in which to draw breath and to find refreshment and renewal I want to begin this journey without any particular pre-conceived goal in mind. It may not all come together immediately; I may be left at the end with questions, loose ends and threads which do not seem to form part of the whole pattern of the tapestry of this time. That is fine. It is risky, counter-cultural, to start out on something with open hands, open mind, open heart, but above all with openness to mystery. We have an image in the Celtic *peregrini*, who set off in their small fragile boats, to go wherever the wind of the spirit might take them, and the goal of their journey was to find 'the place of their resurrection', a phrase which speaks of the true self, the resurrected self – a secret known only to each one of us and to God.

CEW29

We must never forget that we are persons made up of body and mind and spirit, endued with five senses, and that we must come to God with the whole of ourselves. 'The glory of God is man fully alive' – a phrase from St Irenaeus of Antloch that we have probably often seen widely quoted. Thomas Merton, when he was teaching his novices at the Trappist monastery of Gethsemani, was insistent on this, telling them time and again that God is looking for the whole self, the fullness of all our senses, not the truncation of self. Someone complained recently, in words that arrested my attention, that we are for all practical purposes withdrawn from 'the sharpness of being'.[1] It might be useful to reflect on this, to use it as a check to ensure that during this time each of these three elements receives due respect and that I use all my senses. One of the simplest and most immediate questions that I might ask myself is how I eat? Do I eat a meal quickly and casually, without paying respect and attention? It was something that Donald Nicholl learnt from Thich Nath Hanh, who watched the speed with which he tore an orange into segments, putting one after another into his mouth before finishing the previous one. At the end he simply asked Donald Nicholl if he thought that he had really eaten that orange.[2]

I want this retreat to bring me a chance to recover a way of life that is more balanced, more in harmony with itself, more free and fulfilling. I now want to take a moment to consider where I am shut up, limited, not as open and life-filled as I might be.

The psalms express this in a number of ways – that I am trapped in a net, bogged down in mire, and I am to escape as a bird, to jump over a wall, to rejoice as a champion to run his course.

࿐

Am I fully alive – alive in all my senses? Am I living with open eyes and open ears? This is the question that St Benedict asked his disciples in the opening words of the Prologue to his Rule, and it is still today a question for any of us.

> However late, then, it may seem, let us rouse ourselves from lethargy. That is what scripture urges on us when it says: the time has come for us to rouse ourselves from sleep. Let us open our eyes to the light that shows us the way to God. Let our ears be alert to the stirring call of his voice crying to us every day: today if you should hear his voice, do not harden your hearts.[3]

The original Latin words carry a much a sharper sound which gets lost in translation, *apertis oculis . . . attonitis auribus*. Biblical imagery is always there just beneath the surface of the text of the Rule, for St Benedict was soaked with the Scriptures and it is this which adds depth to his words. So this calls the Transfiguration to mind with the scene of drowsy disciples being startled by the shining forth of the brilliant light of Christ, and their ears astonished by a sound like thunder. This is the divine light, the light which not only shows us the way to God but makes us more like God, shapes us into his likeness.

This light of the Transfiguration will be another of the threads that runs through the tapestry of this book. It is both totally mysterious and awesome and yet immediately accessible as we see from a nun of Stanbrook, a community which follows the Rule of St Benedict, when she writes of the daily opening of our eyes to that light from God that will transform our way of seeing.

> We do not have much theory and system. We simply open
> our eyes every day to the light that comes from God and
> trust that light to transform our way of seeing.[4]

Living the life that she does, she tells us that here there are no boundaries between the sacred and the secular for the Rule of St Benedict shows the dignity and value both of people and of things, and
brings into daily life a kind of awe in the presence of the holy.

ᘓ✿ᘐ

Much of this book will be about the sense of awe in the midst
of daily life, about seeing, the art of seeing (which perhaps we
might more usefully think of as the discipline of seeing) or about
the recovery of vision. For this reason I want to suggest making
regular use of a magnifying glass during this retreat. Since I have
begun to make it a part of my ordinary daily life it is almost as
though it has added an extra dimension to the way in which I
now look at the world.[5] It is of course quite wonderful for time
spent out of doors and later on I shall write further about the
practice of walking with attention, awareness. I found myself
astonished when for the first time I picked a daisy and held it
under my magnifying glass. It was particularly exciting for someone whose scientific schooling had been so badly neglected for it
meant that I was totally unprepared to discover, or to uncover,
what I now found – this world virtually invisible to the naked
eye. But it can just as well be used indoors, around the house,
from a hospital bed, when confined to a room. The principle
remains the same: take time and notice what you see. It is important to use whatever comes to hand and stay with it, be happy
with it whatever it may be, do not try to find something better
somewhere else. A few minutes each day is quite enough – perhaps
fitted into a lunch break, or snatched while the children are
sleeping. Living or working in a city does not mean that there
will not be a leaf, a twig, moss between concrete slabs, weeds

pushing up through gravel. Being in hospital means fruit or flowers beside the bedside. The kitchen presents me with utensils or food that I so regularly handle without noticing: a bowl of sugar, the rind of a lemon, the texture of an apple. These are the realities which surround me, and all too often lie neglected under my feet or escape the notice of hands and eyes.

The odes of Pablo Neruda show a delight in things, in the ordinary, daily things, cups and soup tureens, spoons, fabric, nails and coins, things crafted by human hands. He tells us how he will pass through houses and streets touching things:

> Many things gave me completeness
> They did not only touch me
> My hand did not merely touch them,
> but rather,
> they befriended
> my existence.[6]

The eye of the glass reveals without judging or analysing: it simply lights up. I explore what I saw with an almost astonished amazement. It is paradoxical that while the glass narrows down, it simultaneously opens up. It showed me details of varied and delicate intricacy within a harmonious and unified whole. Here were an endlessly imaginative and totally original invention of shapes, with unexpected and hidden internal rhythms. Time and again it would be amusing, odd or absurd. God must have a sense of the absurd to create things so amazingly eccentric. Perhaps he enjoyed just going on playing with shapes – as small children do when they shout 'Let's . . . do this, do that'. From flowers I turned to lichen and fern, moss and leaves, wood and pebbles, and even such unexpected things as bird shit or animal droppings proved to be marvellously put together. Soon I found that I was actually caught up in this new world, and in some extraordinary way it began to teach me about my own self, and about my place in the whole cosmic pattern of the universe.

C❦❦Ɔ

The monastic tradition has always known about finding God in the daily and the ordinary, so it should not really surprise us that in recent years the monastic vision has escaped the cloister and become the property of many lay people who find that it brings them a down-to-earth refreshment of spirit which sadly they often fail to find in the institutional Church. People are waking up to hear the call of the monastery bell – and if we think of that as the bell for the first Office of the day, which is *Vigils*, then we are given the further image of a wake-up call, a call to become vigilant, alert, fully awake, fully alive. An American lay woman, who is fortunate enough to he associated with a Cistercian abbey, describes her experience of the institutional Church as that of finding 'no room at the inn'. But she tells us that when there is no room in the traditional structures, 'God with us' becomes a reality in the stable, on the margins. She is fortunate because she lives within easy distance of a religious community and she is able to spend a day a week there, and to share a life which she says brings her an 'experience of God with the confidence of love, not with the certitude of knowledge and understanding'.[7]

One of the themes of this book, the relationship of the inner and the outer, the connection between my outer environment and my inner life of prayer, would have come very naturally to anyone living in a monastic environment, for it is forcibly expressed in an architectural image which lay at the heart of their daily lives, literally and metaphorically. The cloister is one of the greatest of monastic gifts, and we should marvel not only at its beauty and its aesthetic delight but even more at its significance and what it can tell us about the way in which we shape the pattern of our lives.

The monastic cloister was something that made a powerful impression on me during the years in which I lived at Canterbury, one of the greatest of all the medieval Benedictine communities.

I came to love its glorious cloister, so rightly called in the Middle Ages the gate of heaven. It was something that I was to recapture in a very different form when I returned to live again in the Welsh Borders, where I could walk around the ruined cloisters of the Cistercian abbey at Tintern, or sit in the empty space which had once formed the cloister complex at Dore Abbey. And I reflected on the audacity of a way of life that put uncluttered space, emptiness, at its heart.

The cloisters were of course originally surrounded by the square of vaulted passage ways running round the four sides and serving a strictly practical purpose for the daily horarium or monastic timetable. They formed what was in effect a link line which brought into a relationship all the buildings necessary for the daily needs of the balanced monastic life with its rhythm of body, mind and spirit; work, study and prayer. Here was a holding together of the physical self with its daily demand for food and sleep (the refectory and the dormitory), the intellectual self which needed the stimulus of reading and art (the scriptorium) as well as the application of a careful mind to daily administration and practical affairs (the chapter house), and finally the spiritual self, to be fed by prayer, the *opus Dei*, the work of God in prayer and praise, in the church, which was the anchor, the base-line to everything else.

So everything centred on God. This does not mean that it is a life of exclusion from the world or appreciation of the world; rather it is a 'life drawn on the largest canvas possible'.[8] The carved bosses which decorated the cloisters of the larger communities are magnificent works of art and works of the imagination – drawn from sources which ranged from the Bible to legend and myth, tales from chivalry or the monsters of a wild medieval inventiveness. Here we have a book of life, full, overflowing life in all its splendour, with all its complexity and contradiction, and from which God is never excluded. They have something of the same exuberance which is found in the medieval mystery plays – those great dramas from which nothing is excluded, which show all the heights and depths of life, and which do not attempt to separate the sublime from the grotesque. For although the cloisters are by definition an enclosed space, that empty uncluttered space which a monastic community places at its heart, they were never intended to be closed-off space.

Here is an image which applies to my own self – and one that I hope that the days of retreat that make up this book will allow me to explore more fully. In the complex of my own daily schedule, with all its demands, I am reminded that it is important, and more than that, fundamental and essential, to keep clear, open space in my own heart. This means that in spite of all the demands, the distractions and the difficulties that besiege my time, I shall try to carry a heart of stillness.

Each chapter of this book ends with material for reflection which readers are encouraged to use in whatever way they please: quotations from Scripture, poems, short extracts, are all meant to lead into reflective, prayerful reading, silence. The inspiration for this comes from the ancient monastic practice, applied to the reading of the Scriptures, known as *lectio divina*, which in its literal translation means 'reading God'. It is summed up in a phrase that can be dated to a letter of St Cyprian in 256 which tells us that it was not only his own personal experience but an already accepted tradition: 'You are to be diligent in prayer and in *lectio*; that is how you speak to God and God in turn speaks to you.'[9] Later, in the hands of Guigo the Carthusian in the twelfth century, it was given further shape, described as four steps of the spiritual ladder, four stages, and much has been written most valuably and usefully which is not relevant here. Our concern here, however, is not with anything that makes it too precise, too technical, but the wish to recapture that original impulse that saw reading as leading into reflection, into contemplation, into stillness until finally it explodes, and bursts into a flame of love. Any sentence from the Scriptures is so filled with such a host of meanings that it accords with the taste, the hunger and thirst and longing of each of us. So Guigo here speaks of it terms of fire and thirst:

> Lord, I have sought your face,
> I have meditated long in my heart
> and in my meditation
> there has blazed up an immense fire of longing
>   to know you more.
> Lord, assuage my thirst for I burn with love.
> And it is the grace of contemplation
> which the Lord gives,
> attentive to the very heart of the prayer.[10]

In ancient times when people read to themselves they read aloud, and already that tells me something that could be valuably applied to my own reading: to take time, to approach it with reverent attentiveness, and with an inner prayer-filled readiness to receive what it may yield up as I stay with it – the medieval terminology was to chew it as a cow chews the cud, very slowly, digesting it in the succession of her stomachs, and when she belches a taste of it returns. I might rewrite that for myself as gleaning. But essentially it means to linger, to repeat, to be slow and deliberate and to value the leisurely pace, expecting to be sustained. Perhaps by finding the phrase or the words that arrest me I shall touch a new depth of knowing, a new and deeper contact with God. But again nothing may happen, and that is also perfectly all right. It is like the knowing and making of a friendship which is not to be measured by immediate and out-wardly tangible results. When St Benedict said that on Sundays all should devote the time which was usually given to manual labour to reading, he used the word, *vacent*, which denotes leisure, taking a little vacation, being empty and receptive. This suggests absolutely what I hope may result from taking time with this material: to let go of tension and expectation, and simply to allow ourselves to be drawn uncluttered into the orbit of God.

ᘒᕀᕀᕀᕀᕀ

Wait ... be silent ... be attentive ... wait ... God is here.

In the end it is prayer which allows me to hold everything else in place and which prevents me from being pulled apart, fragmented. The sense of the presence of God is the anchor, the linchpin, the rock, by which all the varied elements of daily life are brought into perspective. Everything flows in and out of prayer: it is as simple as that. Living and praying become one continuous flowing movement, in a life in which each element plays its part in a harmonious and balanced whole. On the inner side of the cloisters the succession of arches cast their shadows in a variety of constantly changing patterns of light and dark, varying according to the times of day or seasons of the year. Here is this further image of the interplay of light and dark, an image which will recur throughout this book.

But there is one further image still. The cloisters enclose a garden or garth in which would stand a fountain or a well. A gardener who visited many of these medieval gardens in order to photograph them was struck by what he called 'a green oasis of safety, simplicity and purity', open to the heavens, funnelling daylight into the heart of the monastery. He reflected on the importance of the green of the grass, but above all on the presence of that running spring which brought a quiet, continuous undercurrent of sound to the whole.[11]

So not only was that inner space within myself to be kept free and uncluttered, but it also had to be watered, refreshed from that fountain at its centre. There are so many different ways of describing this still centre and of interpreting the spring of water. Each of us will have our own picture. Essentially the purpose of that emptiness is that it becomes the space for listening to the Word – we enter into silence and hear God's conversation and take our proper part in it – and if we pay heed to ancient monastic wisdom, we know that that means trying not to say too much ourselves. It is the place of openness and of silence where God finds us and we find him, but it is also a space for listening to others, for a deepening sense of awareness of relatedness to the world.

The picture of the cloister almost inevitably sounds romantic. But it is vital to see the cloister space in my own self as the pivot around which daily life revolves, the rock or anchor which holds it firmly grounded. This is what Christ meant when he said 'Go into your room'. There is a passage written by St Ambrose in the fourth century which makes it quite clear that what Christ had in mind had no reference to a physical place:

> You must not think that he means by this a room with four walls separating you physically from others, but the room that is within you, where your thoughts are shut up, the room that contains your feelings. This room of prayer is with you at all time, wherever you go it is a secret place and what happens there is witnessed by God alone.[12]

This retreat may not only give me the chance to think again about how I might carry this interior space within me but also now I might create a special physical place, however small, set apart as a touchstone or a point of reference, as it were, to which I can return in order to strengthen my commitment to silence and prayer. What shape might it take? This description of how one monk used his cell comes towards the end of this introduction – but in speaking of the importance of gaze and conversation it also takes us forward to what will be important in the rest of this book.

> The corner of his cell where he prayed was his home. Every month or so he would rearrange from his array of lamps, icons, beads, books, cards, flowers, rugs and cushions, but what never changed was the unflagging, unsentimental, heart-felt contemplative gaze and conversation.[13]

The Pattern of the Retreat

I have set out this book as a succession of days or stages but that must be seen as entirely optional. Many people may just pick it up and read it as a book that has no connection with any time-scale or with the pattern of a retreat. That is fine. I hope that each reader will find something different, and that each one will use it in whatever way seems best to them, will adapt it in whatever way suits their particular needs and purpose, and particularly will read it at their own pace. Enjoy what is useful, disregard the rest.

If busy people who want to use it as a retreat guide can only manage a very short time each day that is also fine. What matters most is that it will be time consciously designated as space for God, time which is entered into intentionally. It does not matter if the space and time is peculiar: one of my own favourite places and times is while travelling, and I have a particular fondness for the top of a London bus. Here I find myself on my own and yet part of a temporary community, a group of people unknown to me (except for what is revealed of their lives by their conversations on their mobile phones); I watch a moving landscape which encourages me to think and to pray for a world which holds so much that is secret and hidden – top floors and skylines can be so wonderfully evocative.

I am most anxious not to give the impression that this should be seen as a progression of successive steps, although I would like to think that each chapter leads into the next in a logical succession. For I see it not only as a gradual process, but essentially a *mysterious* process. For it is in the spaces for silence, reflection, and prayer that God will be at work, and how can we possibly know how that will bear fruit? So whatever happens, or does not happen, is in God's hands.

❦

At the end of the seven months that Henri Nouwen spent with the Trappists in the abbey of the Genesee in upstate New York, where he had gone in order to bring some much-needed peace and balance into a frenetic and over-busy life, he told the community that his stay had not only brought him closer to Christ but closer to the world as well. Six months later, when he had returned to his former work, he asked himself what difference this time apart had actually made. He reflected ruefully on how idealistic his hopes had been: 'Somehow I had expected that my restlessness would turn into quietude, my tensions into a peaceful lifestyle.' It is this honesty which makes him so valuable a guide as we stand on the brink of embarking upon this time. 'A monastery is not built to solve problems but to praise the Lord in the midst of them.' Do not expect too much; be open to simple gifts. And what were these gifts for him? He lists them:

the glimpse of God's graciousness that I saw in my solitude,
the ray of light that broke through my darkness,
the gentle voice that spoke in my silence,
the soft breeze that touched me in my stillest hour.[14]

Before we go any further let us ask God to be at work in us during these coming days as we read and pray and look and walk and write.

As we commend ourselves to his grace, we ask in our own words for guidance and support. But we also use the words of that most ancient of prayers which St Benedict took from Cassian, and which since then has been said by countless Christians in every age and every place, adding our voices to those who have recognized that when we turn to God he will uphold and strengthen us:

O God come to my aid
O Lord make haste to help me.

Passages for Reflective Reading
and Prayer

A vast inheritance.

These are the words of John Henry Newman in the introduction to his *Lectures on the Prophetical Office of the Church*, written in 1837. He went on to say that we have 'no inventory of our treasures', and I feel that that still remains sadly true today. We neglect the rich treasury of an inheritance stretching back over the centuries. Yet when we neglect the traditions which belong to us, it is, in the vivid image that the historian Lady Elizabeth Longford liked to use, rather like living in a house without windows.

In the early Fathers, Eastern and Western, the Celtic saints, holy men and women of the Middle Ages, seventeenth-century Anglican mystics – I have included here material from many varied sources – we have a richness of erudition and insight, of wisdom and scholarship, of beautiful and imaginative writing. I look on it as ancient wisdom which is always new, yielding up fresh riches as we approach it with new questions, make new demands. It is a source or spring from which to draw again and again.

The psalms have shaped the daily worship of monastics and many of us know them well through parish life or private prayer – particularly those of us brought up on the *Book of Common Prayer* which provided us with a storehouse of words which have delighted us and continue to haunt our memory. For centuries the psalms have been 'the main channel of spiritual nourishment to innumerable men and women' for here, as Alan Ecclestone says, we have 'words to be absorbed, insights to be observed, songs to be sung, commitments to be made our own'. I have taken this from his Foreword to the new translations of the psalms made by Jim Cotter which is what I have chosen to use to start the selection of quotations and passages for reflection which end each chapter. I have found that simply the unfamiliarity of the words that Jim Cotter uses jolts me, startles me into new perceptions, and into seeing things afresh. He expands them so that they become more like a meditation. I also like what he says about praying them either with an 'I' or with 'we'. 'In the psalms we read soul-deep into the life of a people and the life of individuals. Indeed their minds and hearts swing easily between identifying with the one and then with the many that they could pray as "I" or as "we" with equal facility.' Here is something important to prevent prayer from becoming too inward-looking.

I have not given references to the passages that I quote since I feel that would distract. But details are given in the Acknowledgements and Sources Section at the end of the book. In addition, I have included a very short summary list of those whom I quote in this book, simply setting out the barest details of dates and background, sufficient to put them into some sort of context. My hope is that readers may glimpse here someone or something which they will want to discover further. I have tried to bring together in this tapestry (since this is how I see this book) voices both of prose and poetry, although the distinction of the two is sometimes blurred since I like to set out prose writing in the form of short lines like a prose poem, to encourage slower and more meditative reading.

Prayers and Reflections

I said, O for the wings of a dove,
that I might fly away and be at rest.
I yearn to flee to the mountains,
to make my dwelling in the wilderness.

. . .

your arms are wide and welcoming,
in your presence we are relaxed,
and feel most strangely at home.

Psalm 55

Vacare Deum.
Be free for God.

I have a need
of such a clearance
as the Saviour effected in the temple of Jerusalem
a riddance of the clutter
of what is secondary
that blocks the way
to the all-important central emptiness
which is filled
with the presence of God alone.

Jean Danielou

'The Kingdom of heaven in mystically within you.'
These are the good things which are hidden within us
and which shine out from within us
by means of the life lived in stillness;
the person who has committed himself to God in faith
and prayer
will no longer be tormented by concern for himself.

Isaac of Syria

I am by nature
an out-of-doors
sort of woman,
a walker, a gardener.
But today,
sitting by the window
in comfortable chair,
watching wind
make white dogwood dance
with blue spruce,
seeing petals
from an ornamental tree
fall like pink confetti,
relishing every movement
of spring's emerald symphony,
I realize I am content
to be inside looking out,
know I can only live
this interior life,
wonder how deep
the tap root
of my heart is.

Bonnie Thurston

Each of us needs an opportunity to be alone,
and silent,
to find space in the day or in the week,
just to reflect
and to listen to the voice of God
that speaks deep with us.
Our search for God is only our response
to his search for us.
He knocks at our door,
but for many people their lives are too
preoccupied
for them to be able to hear.

Cardinal Basil Hume

You are near Lord,
The Lord is near to all of us,
because he is everywhere.
We cannot escape him . . .
nor deceive him . . .
nor lose him . . .
God watches everything,
he sees everything.
He is close to each one of us;
as he says:
I am a God who is close at hand.

St Ambrose

This is the reason
why we have no ease of heart or soul,
for we are seeking our rest in trivial things,
                              which cannot satisfy,
and not seeking to know God,
almighty, all-wise, all-good.
He is true rest.

Julian of Norwich

When the time for silence comes, I ask you to take up your position for prayer (and sitting is usually best for most of us) and then, having asked the help of the Holy Spirit, to be content to wait patiently, expectantly, lovingly, longingly. Try to realize that this is all you you can do for yourself. God must do the rest. See yourself as the parched ground looking upwards waiting patiently for the rain to fall. You can only wait.

Fr Roger Schultz of Taizé

God is everywhere
utterly vast,
and everywhere near at hand,
according to his own witness of himself;
I am, he says, a God at hand
and not a God afar off.
The God we are seeking
is not one who dwells far away from us;
we have him within us.

St Columbanus

2

Seeing with the Inner Eye

The riches of my own interior landscape have, particularly in more recent years, gained as much from the visual as from the verbal, from image as well as word, from poetry as well as prose. One of my main concerns in this book therefore has been to share the role that I have myself found that the imagination can play, and to show how its cultivation can bring about 'a transfiguring encounter':

> transforming human lives into the likeness of Christ. By taking our imagination captive, the Spirit reshapes our desires, our hopes, our values, our way of seeing the world, and thereby reshapes human living. Rediscovering the imagination, therefore, is an important step in learning how to respond to what God is doing to our own lives and in the world around us.[1]

Thomas Merton always insisted on the part that the imagination should play in the spiritual life:

> Imagination is the creative task of making symbols, joining things together in such a way that they throw new light on each other and on everything around them. The imagination is a discovering faculty, a faculty for seeing relationships, for seeing meanings that are special and even quite new.[2]

The longer that we stay with an image and dialogue with it, the more will it yield up. 'A symbol should go on deepening' as

Flannery O'Connor says.[3] We have to wait for the image to find us. Sometimes it may come unbidden, but often we must expect to stay with it, and to be ready to go deeper, layer upon layer, always waiting expectantly. Images are best described in images – as *footholds* into a truth that cannot be expressed fully in words. Some of the images may be familiar, others strange. Sometimes time seems frozen, at other times fluid. Sometimes they come suddenly and easily, and then, as the Ulanovs warn as they write of *The Healing Imagination*, they depart suddenly just when we most wanted to hold on to them:

> Either way, they speak of another life running in us like an underground river-current, always present, never quite seen, exerting influence on us lapping quietly on our dry ground, rich soil from which things grow.[4]

Rowan Williams, like Merton both poet and theologian, speaks of it as an unveiling – something that may be startling, risky:

> When we move with poetry and the imagination,
> when we deal with symbols and images,
> we become people
> who are happy with mystery
> and open to discovery.
> To deepen the mystery,
> to embrace complexity is risky.
> We need to have courage
> enough to be ready for an unveiling
> which can be a startling process.[5]

This is something that the Orthodox world has always known. In the Eastern church we find a tradition that does not deal so much with the cerebral, with what can be grasped by the intellect, but believes that the grace and truth of God can enter into our souls as much by the eye as by the ear. This is one of the reasons that icons play such an important part both in private prayer and in public worship. I too have come to appreciate the art of the icon; I have found as Thomas Merton did, that icons 'open out onto what *is*'. But it is interesting to remind ourselves, and also perhaps to take comfort from the fact that for him this was not always so. At his first encounter not only did they mean nothing, he actually saw them simply as 'little irate Byzantine-looking saints with beards and great haloes' who seemed to him merely 'clumsy, ugly and brutally stupid'. Yet when he died in Bangkok in 1968, amongst the very few personal possessions that accompanied his body home on the army plane was one small icon on wood of the Virgin and child. It had been given to him a few years previously and it has been part of his life ever since. It was for Merton, as he wrote to his Greek Orthodox friend who had given it to him, like a kiss from God:

> It is a perfect act of timeless worship.
> I never tire of gazing at it . . .
> it is unutterably splendid
>   And silent.

He found that it imposed a silence on the whole of his hermitage.[6] If icons are to play a part in this retreat it is important to treat them with the sense of reverence that we find here. Their popularity in recent years, the way in which we can now so easily find ourselves surrounded by a plethora of icons, poor reproductions, perhaps even faded and neglected, hanging in rooms and corridors in so many places, militates against them being what they really should be. We need to take time with them, silent time, allow what they are speaking of, which is beyond words, to enter into our hearts, penetrate our innermost being, and lead us into those depths where our God-given life is struggling to grow.

The art of the icon catches the gaze of God in a way that no other expression, whether by word or image, could possibly do. A whole world opens, a world which reveals God's utter strangeness and yet simultaneously his immediacy, his vulnerability. It is as though here we touch the nearness yet the otherness of the

Eternal. The mysterious power of the icon is that by taking us
into this world we find that mystery is not far away 'but hidden
within each one of us, closer to us than our own heart'.[7]

An icon reminds us to balance the gift of hearing, listening,
with that of looking, seeing. In an icon of the Annunciation, for
example, we are reminded that not only did Mary hear the message of the angel but there was also the meeting of the eyes: the
enraptured gaze of angel and woman with the dove of the Holy
Spirit spinning the thread of their mutual gaze:

> These neither speak nor movement make
> But stare into their deepening trance
> As if their gaze would never break.[8]

We cannot fully appreciate the icon unless we begin with the
eyes. Icons depend on the eyes. When they 'show a way', they
invite us to make a little journey into the picture, the journey
that the eye has to make around the whole complex image. Then
we find ourselves caught up in the interchange of eyes, the gaze
that passes, in a circular motion, from one figure to another –
the gaze of love. It is found above all in that very familiar icon
by Rublev of the Trinity. Here we see three figures whose bodies
are gently and insistently inclined towards one another, listening
intently, the hair drawn back from their ears, but also looking at
one another, with 'listening eyes', with a deeply compassionate
gaze which expresses the depth of their love. There are no shadows
here for divine light permeates everything; everything is flooded
with pure, profound love. And the reverse perspective of the icon
draws us in so that we do not stand outside as spectators but are
invited in to share this perfect communion.

We also see it in those icons known as the *hodegritia*, in which
the Christ child sits cradled on his mother's left arm, and his
eyes take us to her face, and to her eyes which are turned outwards
towards us. But her gesture tells us not to keep our eyes on her but
to look to her child. He is looking at her and so he draws us back
to her face, that face which is the object of his own loving gaze.

Mary addresses us with her eyes, eyes which in his poem 'Our Lady of Vladimir' Rowan Williams calls 'her immeasurable eyes' as he catches for us the intensity of her love:

> O how he clings, see how
> he smothers every pore, like the soft
> shining mistletoe to my black bark,
> she says, I cannot breathe, my eyes
> are aching so.[9]

It will hardly be surprising to learn that I have found that poetry has a most important part to play in this retreat. As Andrew Motion says, a poem will touch our deepest feelings: will make us feel, make us explore.[10] When Merton introduced his novices to the work of Rilke he called a poem a work of encounter in which 'something explodes'. Since he was himself a poet as well as a monk, he knew something of the art of the poet and what it was that was needed to make a good poem effective. In a poor poem, he told them, where the ego gets in the way, we might learn about the poet's feelings; in a good poem, where there will be straight encounter, it is as though the poet makes us also an artist. It is like a process by which we become a partner in a conversation, or a participant in an exploration, and we begin to see and to understand what hitherto we had been unable to articulate. Then it may happen that a poem will express something that we had been half aware of feeling but unable to put into words. A poet can give a name to what otherwise 'might dwell unknown in the heart'.[11]

For poetry deals in paradox and ambiguity, it works allusively and metaphorically, choosing words which startle and surprise, so that much is merely hinted at or left unsaid. A good poem does not limit or exhaust the realities of which it speaks. So I wait and allow it to reveal itself to me, for a poem comes to life only when I am fully attentive, and this may mean being prepared to hear it a number of times. But then there comes a moment of discovery, a shock of recognition, which relates these words to my own experience in such a way that they open up a new realm of understanding or insight. Poetry can capture 'briefly but uniquely, moments of recognition and epiphany' and new journeys begin with such moments, journeys for which the poem becomes an agent of transformation.[12]

A man who has travelled widely giving public recitals makes a more dramatic claim: he says that reading poetry is a fierce and dangerous practice, that good poetry has the power to start a fire in your life, that it can alter the way you see the world and you may never be the same again. And if, as he warns, 'it dares us to break free from the safe strategies of the cautious mind', surely that is exactly why it has such a vital role to play in any spiritual exploration?[13]

If poetry is to form any part of this retreat we must remember that poetic language, unlike most of the words which assault and batter us today, is not exhausted on first hearing. Instead we should perhaps treat it in the same way that the monastic tradition teaches us the art of *lectio divina*, taking time, reading slowly, possibly reading aloud, savouring the words fully, taking delight in them, lingering over certain phrases – finding the spaces between words. I like to remind myself of Mary pondering in her heart what she did not immediately understand – the Latin *pondus*, weight, giving us the clue: to hold something precious like a stone in the hand, feeling its weight, letting it communicate its essence to us. This is an exercise not unlike the practice of walking with attentiveness – holding words and phrases as we would the objects we find on the path, and taking the time as we continue to hold them in order to allow our attention to become attuned to what is *there*.

... and God is the poetry caught in any religion caught but not imprisoned.[14]

These lines which come from the Australian poet Les Murray echo something that Merton knew and wanted to tell the young men aspiring to become monks. He said that they should think of poetry as analogous to religion, bringing them into touch with reality, with God. We come alive through reality and God mediates himself through that reality, whether in creation, or in daily life. He then went on to warn them that this could be a catapult into the unknown, it might be unsafe. 'Are you ready for it?' he asked them.[15]

Poets and artists have always shown us that 'the observed particulars take on the mystery of revelation'. That is why I have a particular fondness for the Chilean poet Pablo Neruda when he tells us:

> I love things with a wild passion,
> extravagantly,
> I cherish tongs,
> and scissors
> I adore cups. ...
> I love all things,
> not only the grand,
> but also the infinite
> -ly
> small.

His list encourages me to make my own list, and to say to myself, as he does:

> I pass through houses,
> streets,
> elevators,
> touching things;
> Many things give me completeness.[16]

Might this time of retreat give me the opportunity not only to read poetry and to think about the place of poetry in my life but also to write some poetry? It will be for myself alone, and for God – an attempt to explore in words and thereby to articulate, things which might otherwise remain half-noticed, half-understood. I might even try to make it a daily discipline, finding something which catches my attention, translating it into an image which tells me more about itself and about my own self, my reaction, my relation to it. Many people know the *haiku* which has become a very popular form in recent years, but there is also in Japan another form, the *tanka*, which I have come to appreciate. It is longer (5, 7, 5, 7, 7) and as a result allows a wider exploration of ideas because it becomes possible to juxtapose two images, to explore contrasts, to search for meaning. Having a set form ready to hand is like having a net, a framework, in which to trap words and it is easy to get into the habit of carrying a notebook, or at least a scrap of paper, and then to try to catch that momentary glimpse, the hint, the elusive moment of beauty or mystery or pain or amusement. Here I wanted to express something of the subtle beauty of the south west of Ireland:

> Soft grey Irish mist
> Enclosing my whole landscape
> But when I reach out
> My hands feel those secret gifts
> Tenderly wrapped and hidden.

Then, in contrast, spending time waiting in an airport and watching planes taking off:

> Huge, slow, earth-bound whales
> Wheeling with great dignity
> Quick transformation
> They become like swallows lifting
> Light and free into the sky.

This is a theme to which I shall return time and again, in the context both of silence and attentiveness – the urgency of *seeing*, seeing anew, seeing with eyes washed clear by contemplative prayer, seeing with eyes cleansed by tears, but above all seeing with delight and wonder. Thomas Traherne, the seventeenth-century Anglican religious poet, until comparatively recently known only to a very few people, opens up a whole new world of seeing which is best described as seeing with delight, a glorious word which carries a lightness about it and seems to be saying: this thing is good, and I am good, and I am happy with my relationship to this world around me, but above all I am happy with my relationship to myself, to my own inwardness, and also to my own outwardness. It is the relationship of the inward and the outward which will recur time and again in this book. Is it anxiety more than delight that compels us so often to use those tools of self-analysis and personality tests? One of the purposes of this time of retreat is not only that I should delight in the world but also discover and delight in my own inwardness. God took delight in his creation, and surely I should do the same – seeing myself as God sees me, with the same delight. Do I yet believe in the delight – full-ness of my own self? And yet also draw back and realize that in the end I am mystery.

The imagination, images, icons, poetry, silence, all bring me to reclaim mystery and above all 'the reality and freshness of God as Mystery', in the words of Mark Oakley who then goes on to say 'theology of this sort is never neat and comfortable but neither is the life under God of which it attempts to speak'.[17] I hope that this retreat will not be neat and comfortable, but will mean hints and guesses, will face us with ambiguity and ambivalence. That is the place where I find myself and I guess that I am not alone.

In my case the external and the interior mirror one another in a way that I cannot escape, for I live in a border country where different voices meet and mingle. Here there is no possibility of the luxury of certainty; I can never feel that I have arrived at some simple and definitive truth. The Jesuit William Johnston describes it in his own situation, that of living in proximity to Buddhism:

> because I am listening to these two choruses
> I will begin to ask questions . . .
> The most that we might hope for
> is God might for a moment unveil himself –
> and that could be as terrifying
> and as unexpected
>   as the Transfiguration.[18]

ॐ

'I will begin to ask questions.' I hope that curiosity will be a propelling force during this time. If our religion is to be alive in our lives it must be a matter of both comfort and discomfort. I must go on asking questions. Rilke made the connection between loving the questions and living into them, and it is important to return again to this familiar passage for it is very apposite at the start of this time:

> I want to beg you as much as I can . . . to be patient towards all that is unsolved in your heart and to try to love the questions themselves . . . Do not now seek answers which cannot be given you because you would not be able to live them. And the point is to live everything. Live the questions now. Perhaps you will then, gradually, without noticing it, live along some distant day into answer.[19]

ॐ

The eye of the glass which I mentioned before is like the eye of the poet. The twentieth-century Welsh poet Saunders Lewis takes one of the commonest flowers of all, in his poem 'A Daisy in April'. It is as though he is seeing it, in spite of it being so familiar, for the first time:

> Yesterday, I saw a daisy
> Like a shining mirror of the dawn.

The previous day he had walked over it without thought. But then he sees, and he sees into its great golden centre, and he sees beyond it to its relationship with the heavens, and he sees, as it opens up, that it reveals the hidden sun at its heart. We have moved into images, and our vision expands. The little sun growing in the grass is looking up towards the great sun high in the sky; the great is reflected in the small, and the small holds within itself the reflection of the great. A million suns lie scattered at our feet and we trample on them heedlessly until we start to *see*.

> The field where the April cuckoo sang
> Has become the milky way:
> The firmament turned upside down
> Millions of the suns in the heavens
> Are placed beneath my feet,
> To gild the grass of this grey earth . . .
> Stars like seraphim
> In the splendid azure sky.
> Yesterday I saw a daisy.[20]

'Surprise is the starting point. It is one of God's more glorious gifts', the Benedictine monk Brother David Stendhal-Rast tells us. The gift of the glass is one of endless surprise. It is only too easy to say the words 'Lost in wonder' without stopping to think that in fact they mean that if I am lost, even just for one tiny instant, I am carried out of myself, experiencing something beyond myself. G. K. Chesterton once said that although wonders would never be lacking in this world, *wonderment* will. And in one of his morning broadcasts Eric James summed it all up for me when he told us to

> Re-discover the wondering heart.

Prayers and Reflections

In the depths of my being you are my God,
at the rising of the sun I seek your face.
My heart thirsts for you, my flesh longs for you,
in a barren and dry land where no water is.

I search for you in unexpected places,
at the edge of the known, in the language of
dreams,

. . .

There may I look long and lovingly,
there may I listen for the word beyond words,
there may I wait for a glimpse of your glory.

Psalm 63

I put my question to the earth, and it replied, 'I am not he';
I questioned everything it held, and they confessed the same.
I questioned the sea and the great deep,
And the teeming live creatures that crawl,
And they replied,
'We are not God; seek higher.'
I questioned the gusty winds,
And every breeze with all its flying creatures told me,
'I am not God.'
To the sky I put my question, to sun, moon, stars,
but they denied me: 'We are not the God you seek.'
And to all things which stood around the portals of my
    flesh I said,
'Tell me of my God.

I am here in this solitude before you,
and I am glad because you see me here.
For, it is here, I think, that you want to see me
and I am seen by you.
My being here is a response you have asked of me,
to something I have not clearly heard.
But I have responded . . .
You have called me here
to be repeatedly born in the Spirit as your child.
Repeatedly born in light,
in unknowing,
in faith,
in awareness,
in gratitude,
in poverty,
in presence,
and in praise.

> Thomas Merton, *A Prayer to God the Father*
> *on the Vigil of Pentecost*

Passive I lie, looking up through leaves,
An eye only, one of the eyes of earth
That open at a myriad points at the living surface.
Eyes that earth opens see and delight
Because of the leaves, because of the unfolding of the
    leaves,
The folding, veining, imbrication, fluttering, resting,
The green and deepening manifold of the leaves.

> Kathleen Raine

You are not he, but tell me something of him.'
Then they lifted up their mighty voices and cried,
'He made us.'
My questioning was my attentive spirit, and their reply,
 their beauty.

St Augustine, *Confessions* X.6,9

In the body there is a little shrine.
In that shrine there is a lotus.
In that lotus there is a little space.
What is it that lives in that little space?
The whole universe is in that little space,
because the creator,
the source of it all,
is in the heart of each one of us.

Parable from the *Upanishads*

3

Silence

'Silence is so accurate.' In a pithy phrase a twentieth-century artist, Mark Rothko, comments on the work of the seventeenth-century still-life artist Chardin, whose paintings invite us into a world of structured stillness and silence. It is as though he can create a sense of suspended time, utter immobility, which he allows us to share with him. And this he achieves by taking the most ordinary and commonplace of scenes and revealing something of the intangible spiritual dimension which underlies them.[1] Being drawn into the quiet depths of the things which immediately surround me but which so often I fail to see, is a good starting point for what I want to think about today – the recovery of silence. Here is one of the most immediate and the most powerful of instruments for deepening and enriching my life – one which I neglect at my peril but one which I might want to evade since it could be frightening to encounter this interior silence which lies at the root of being. As Rothko says, silence is so accurate.

For it is very easy to talk about silence, and to read the numbers of attractive books on silence. This, however, can become a way of escaping its demands and reality, for words about silence might become simply another consumer acquisition, one more tool for the spiritual life that we acquire and keep in stock on our bookshelves. That is why it is good to turn to the artists, poets and writers who have always known this as a vital element of their creative work. At some level I also know it myself. Yet at another level I always find it surprisingly difficult to let go of the busyness and the distractions and movement in order to be still and to create stillness around me for any real length of time. Apparently Thomas Merton once said to a friend that in silence 'we must simply realize that we are in water over our head'.[2] I have no means of knowing if Merton was in some subconscious way thinking of the waters of the womb here, but for me the phrase conjures up darkness and coming to birth, and not least the frightening and risky prospect of finding what may open up from that still and silent centre.

African people use the expressive word *mzungu* to describe the white people whom they observe as always being so restless, unable to sit still for long, rushing round in circles, moving from one thing to another. Monasticism, whether Christian or not, emphasizes the role of stillness. Physical stillness precedes the stilling of the mind, and the body plays an essential part here. Eastern religions with their long experience of the art of sitting have much to teach us. For each of us during this time of retreat it is important to discover what is most comfortable and most natural for our own selves. It is not about being heroic, comparing or competing or achieving. I love that gentle advice which tells us to find the position most comfortable in which to sit perfectly still

> as if we do not wish to disturb a bird
> that has flown down and is resting on our head.

Next comes the matter of breathing. This again has been carefully explored in all religious cultures. We know how important it is to be attentive, though with a relaxed attentiveness, giving full attention to each breath yet without any self-conscious awareness of oneself as being the breather. Perhaps counting will help at the start, first one as the in-breath and two as the out-breath. How basic this is. Just sitting gives me a strong sense of rootedness.

But it is even more than this: breath is life itself. To be aware of my breathing is to be aware of life. Breath and spirit are one in the Hebrew word *ruah*. What amazing generosity of a God to give us this gift which we have in abundance throughout our lives and yet can so easily take for granted. Then, as I stay consciously with my breath, I may begin to see this gentle rhythm of breathing in and then breathing out again as a microcosm of my whole life: that first breath which I took in at birth; that last breath that I shall take when I die and give my life back to God.

In a typical aphorism, Thomas Merton who allows profundity to sit side by side with jocularity famously said:

> What I do is live
> How I pray is breathe.[3]

'All arts are derived from the breath that God breathed into the human body.' Hildegard of Bingen knew that whereas breathing is for the most part unconscious, in singing one has to take control of the breath and to become aware of it. When she introduced long phrases into her music, the breath of the physical self became a living metaphor for the Holy Spirit and so each act of breathing can be an act of experiencing the divine. At this point I should stop reading and take a moment or two to notice my own breathing. Then I might try to breathe from the deepest parts of my being. It is a good idea, if it is possible, to sing something aloud. An author who is a musician and who has studied Hildegard can help us here:

> Breathe deep, breathe deep,
> Feel the movement of the life in your body;
> Feel the circling of the blood, the beat of the heart;
> Feel the digestive juices breaking down the food into
> nourishment;
> Breathe deep, breathe deep.
>
> Breathe deep . . . deep . . . deep . . .
> Feel the air . . . flowing freely . . . freely . . . freely

In and out ... in and out ... the rhythm ... the rhythm of
   living.

Living ... living ... your living ... our living
Breathe deep, breathe deep ...
Breathe ... breathe ... breathe.[4]

૨૯❦૭૭

Already in the *Philokalia*, that collection of early monastic texts
on prayer of the heart, the power of attending to the breath was
recognized:

> You know, brother, how we breathe;
> we breathe the air in and out.
> On this is based the life of the body
> and on this depends its warmth.
> So,
> sitting down in your cell,
> collect your mind,
> lead it to the path of the breath along which the air
>   enters in,
> constrain it to enter the heart,
> and keep it there.[5]

Even if I manage no more than ten minutes of sitting still at
the start of each day (or if a work schedule or other demands
make that impossible, at some regular point during the day), then
I will have made a commitment to a time of silence which will
play an important part in so much that I want to explore in
words and images and reflective praying.

> Listen to the silence,
> let it enfold you,
> like a piece of music,
> like bird-watching.

These words are ones that I have often used at the start of a time of retreat since they remind us how vital it is that we do not try to *use* a time of silence but instead simply let it enfold us.

ᘇᙒ᙭ᘏᘙ

I want to turn at this point to painters and see how they help me to understand this. Thomas Merton pays homage to what he gained from his own father, a landscape painter. He tells us in the early pages of his autobiography, *The Seven Storey Mountain*, about growing up in the south of France with an artist father who loved and understood that landscape as Cezanne had done. What is peculiarly distinctive about Owen Merton's canvases, exhibited in London galleries in the 1930s to the acclaim of the critics, is how uncrowded they are. He leaves empty space so that it is as though he invites the viewer in to share his experience. It was a vision that his son said showed veneration for the place and for 'all the circumstances that impress an individual identity on each created things'. He called this a vision that was religious and clean:

> His paintings were without decoration or superfluous comment, since a religious man respects the power of God's creation to bear witness for itself. My father was a very good artist.[6]

When we look at Cezanne's watercolours of Provence we find them much lighter, almost lyrical compared to his larger and more familiar paintings. Here he is spare in his approach to paint, never wanting to overcrowd the space, happy with a broken, dissolving vision, of which Rilke once said that the blank areas of the paper stood not for absence but rather for presence.

The artists' eyes have shown us through their work a visual sense of the emptiness of silence, empty space in which we can become aware of the presence of God. I now turn this into a prayer for my busy, cluttered, noisy way of life:

Uncrowd my heart, O God,
until silence speaks
in your still, small voice;
turn me from the hearing of words,
and the making of words,
and the confusion of much speaking,
to listening,
waiting,
stillness,
silence.

ℭℰ✻ℑℐ

One of Merton's earlier books is *Silence in Heaven* in which he asks what the monastic vocation involves and then answers in words which are rather more romantic and flowery than we find in his later writing but nonetheless give us thought for meditation:

We are called to enter into the hiddenness and the
                    silence of God.
Do we think we know what that means?

                    . . .

Words are only the threshold of the mystery
and the silence of God's love,
selecting a soul for this strange life
hidden in Himself,
is too vast an ocean
to be lapped up by the human tongue.[7]

Whether in cloister or in choir he saw his vocation as always being a call to sink deep roots in the silence of God. The value of the Daily Office is drawn not so much from its sound as from the deep silence of God which enters into that sound and gives it meaning. Monastic life was thus a life wholly centred upon this tremendous existential silence of God which nobody has ever been able to explain and which is, nevertheless, the heart of all that is real. Even though it is right to insist that this silence cannot be explained, nevertheless we must never forget its reality, and even though we cannot grasp the whole substance of the mystery, we can still catch glimpses of its hidden depths.

> Only the everlasting silence in things is real:
> for it is the silence of God,
> buried in their very substance,
> singing the song which he alone can hear.

❦

As the silence opens up in our hearts, and as we listen to it, it is as though we begin to feel the secret presence of the Word expanding 'like a marvellous hidden smile'. Merton then quotes from Isaac of Stella, the twelfth-century Cistercian:

> Let the Son of God grow in thee,
> for He is formed in thee.
> let Him become immense in thee,
> and may He become a great smile
> and exultation and perfect joy.[8]

❦

The art of silence is an art form which, like the art of seeing, is virtually neglected in the West (except that recent years have seen a growing interest in the practice of meditation). Traditional societies, however, have always known the importance of silence. The Australian aboriginal word for it is *dadirri*, and an Australian priest says of it that it means 'the open-eyedness of someone who explores where he or she has always belonged'. It is that sense of *belonging* in the silence that strikes me: is this a gift which primal people show me so that I may recover something which is primal to my own self?

The Christian aboriginal artist, Miriam-Rose Ungummer, calls it tapping into a deep spring that is within us all. 'When I experience "dadirri" I am made whole again' she tells us:

> My people are not threatened by silence.
> They are completely at home with it . . .
>
> I can find peace in this silent awareness.
> There is no need of words.
> There is no need to reflect too much
> and to do a lot of thinking.
> It is just being aware.
> Our aboriginal culture has taught us to be still and to
> > wait.

This is waiting on God, and it cannot be hurried:

> There is nothing more important
> than what we are attending to
> There is nothing more urgent that we must hurry
> > away to.
> We wait on God.
> His time is the right time.
> We wait for him to make his word clear to us.
> We know that in time
> and in the spirit
> of deep listening
> and quiet stillness
> His way will be clear.[9]

This is a constant refrain of the psalms, repeated time and time again. It is the call to be alert, listening, waiting, in silent awareness and stillness for that is how we shall find God.

> Be still before the Lord.
> And wait in patience. (Ps. 36.7)

Vacate et videte quoniam ego sum deus.

The Latin of Psalm 46 lends itself to alternative translations:

Be still and know that I am God.

Empty yourself and know that I am God.

෴

Silence is not absence but presence. Like Elijah in the cave I find that God is here in 'the sound of sheer silence' (to use the words of a recent translation) – God present in this total stillness. Silence and stillness are gifts which are gentle, fragile, to be handled with care, above all in allowing time to wait and to listen. For silence is to lead into listening. St Benedict says quite simply 'the disciple should be silent and listen'. To listen means to be open, ready to receive, attentive to something or to someone outside of myself:

> There is a higher kind of listening
> which is not an attentiveness to a particular
>   wavelength
> a receptivity to a certain kind of message,
> but a general emptiness that waits to realize the
>   message of God
> within our own particular void.

And then Thomas Merton, who spent so much of his life exploring silence, and who in his writings showed that it was neither escapist nor irrelevant for any of us, has this warning – that we should not prepare our minds for any particular message that we might like to hear but just remain empty:

> because I know that I can never expect or anticipate
> the word that will transform my darkness into light.
> I do not even anticipate a special kind of
> transformation.
> I do not demand light instead of darkness.
> I wait on the Word of God in silence
> and when I am 'answered',
> it is not so much by a word that bursts into my silence,
> it is by my silence itself suddenly,
> inexplicably revealing itself to me as a word of great power,
> full of the voice of God.[10]

It was in his monastic community at Gethsemani that Merton learnt the role of silence, for this is something that the Cistercians have always known, from their origins in the twelfth century when they returned to what they saw as the essentials of the Rule and made it central to their monastic practice. It has remained so ever since. David Tomlins, the abbot of the Australian Cistercian monastery at Tarrawarra, sees it as vital for all Christians today:

> The most deafening voice is our own. Desires, fears, anxieties and obsessive worries, a treadmill of thoughts, issuing from a constantly chattering mind.[11]

It means that we learn to nurture a silence not only of the lips and of the heart but even more urgently a silence of the mind. There are tapes that play themselves over and over again, establishing their tyranny over us as they encourage us to return to unresolved situations and conversations. There are straying thoughts which pull us in all directions; there are negative thoughts that subtly invade and then drag us down. Dealing with this has been a constant preoccupation of Christian writers for centuries, for in this case the human psyche changes little. Much that is valuable and illuminating has been written about the subject and this is not the place to deal with it at any length. But a wise and experienced woman recently said this, and a brief quotation provides some helpful advice:

> Watchfulness of thoughts is the practice of catching a thought, perception, or feeling, at its first inkling ... when we watch our thoughts we anticipate and are on the alert for thoughts ... that may become afflictions ... Watchfulness of thoughts is a practice of simple awareness, noticing and letting thoughts come 'as they are' without resistance or editing. Then we simply let them go. A thought will go away by itself if we don't accompany that thought with another thought ... for when we couple that thought with the next thought we give it life.[12]

The basic motivation for guarding the heart and for watchfulness of thoughts is to create an attitude and a capacity for cultivating a listening silence, attentive listening, or in a phrase used by James Finley, *expectant listening*. He applied it to how we read, and described the art of reading in silence as 'attentive expectancy'. He said that it demanded the same care as that exercised by someone searching for lost treasure in a forest:

> We read in silence; we read looking for God. But we read in a particular way. A man drops a rare diamond in the leaves of the forest floor. Carefully, he kneels down. One by one he lifts each leaf. Slowly he searches, knowing his lost treasure is in the leaves. And this is how it is that we must read, listen to another and wait in silence ... In silence there is no routine, for in silence everything is all at once. Everything is new.[13]

☙❧

In the Prologue when St Benedict quotes Psalm 98.4–5, 'Today if you should hear his voice harden not your hearts', it carries an echo of his earlier words when he spoke of 'the ear of the heart'. This is an image that I love for it is a warning about a hardened heart, a heart which is lacking in sensitivity and vulnerability. This is of course a common scriptural metaphor, popular with the Fathers. One of the sayings of the Desert Fathers tells how Abbot Poimen, when asked about hardness of heart, said:

> Water is by nature soft,
> stone on the contrary hard.
> But when water drips continually on a stone,
> it hollows it out.
> So too,
> God's Word is delicate and mild,
> our heart on the contrary hard.
> Yet whoever hears the Word of God frequently and reflects
> on it,
> makes space within his heart,
> so that it can enter in.

> We believe that the divine presence
> is everywhere
> and that in every place
> the eyes of the Lord are watching.

But if God is gazing on us so we too should be gazing on him. John of Forde, the twelfth-century English Cistercian, uses this amazingly simply sentence to describe prayer:

> Gaze silently on the Word.[14]

The commitment to the time of prayer is the keystone to this retreat. It is so easy and attractive to read about prayer and to talk about prayer. But unless we go to pray there is no prayer. There must be a simple desire for God. After his death we learnt the secret which lay at the heart of Cardinal Basil Hume's public life. During the homily that he gave at the requiem mass the present Abbot of Ampleforth, Timothy Wright, said this:

> He was determined to give God every morning, every day . . . This makes it sound so easy, and at one level it is. You do not require a degree in spirituality, nor a stunning religious experience before you can start. You just have to be determined to give time to God every day. Those moments, silent, alone, before God, gave him the strength to be loving and understanding of others. He understood how difficult it was to keep it going, he could sympathize with us in our difficulties and doubts; he knew what it was to feel incompetent in prayer . . .
>
> It was these years of persevering prayer, early each morning which brought him face to face with his own weaknesses. He learnt he had to depend on God . . .
>
> He learnt that there were no short-cuts in prayer. There is only one answer: to keep going in spite of everything, in spite of weakness, failure, distractions, boredom.
>
> In silent prayer he opened himself to the God who gave him so much, and from whom he learnt the real truth about himself and about his vocation.[15]

Sheila Cassidy tells us very honestly about the way in which she starts each day in silence and prayer. She gets up at 6.15 a.m. and with a mug of tea, which she clasps to herself like a comforter, she sits cross-legged on the floor in front of an icon and a candle. Turning a big hour-glass upside down she abandons the hour to God:

This is waste-of-time, holocaust prayer. I often feel really lousy, tired, nauseated, dreadful and long to creep back to bed, but I do not because this is God's time, not mine, and I know that its quality lies not in what I feel but in the totality of my gift. This is a time of abandonment to God, a time in which I try to still my mind and just be open, receptive to him. My prayer is totally without images and largely without words.

She tells us that after twenty years this emptying of the mind comes relatively easily to her, and that if her mind is invaded by a kaleidoscope of thoughts and ideas she simply ignores them – or if they are too insistent to be ignored she will gather them up and include them in her prayer.[16]

In her case she places a candle and an icon to give a focus to her place of prayer. This is worth thinking about. It will be different for each person. It does not matter how simple it is provided that we treat it with respect and do not take it for granted. It might be a good idea to re-arrange it at intervals but what is unchanging is that it is a reflection of commitment to the time of stillness and silence, that we are ready, as St John of the Cross simply says, 'to be still in God, fixing our loving attention upon him'.

> O God,
> I commend to you this time
> and ask you to bless
> and to strengthen me
> in my heartfelt search
> for that silence and stillness
> in which I pray
> I shall find you
> and you will find me.

Prayers and Reflections

I have calmed and quickened my whole being,
I am like a child contented at the mother's breast,
in the stillness I look into the eyes of my lover,
I am absorbed in the task of the moment.

It is like the silence of an evening in spring,
made intense by the bleat of a lamb.
It is like the waves of the sea come to rest,
no more than a whisper in the caress of the shore.

The silence and stillness lift the woodsmoke of prayer.

Psalm 131

This flower,
this light,
this moment,
this silence –
The Lord is here.
Best because the flower is itself,
and the silence is itself,
and I am myself.

Thomas Merton

Prayer is not
scrabbling together
a few paltry words,
flinging them like stones
at the windows
of ineffability.

It is *Gelassenheit*,
   letting go,
being carried on a current
toward a vast ocean,
deep beyond imagining;

sitting silently,
gaze firmly fixed
on one golden,
inscrutable face,
waiting
with the patience of love;

pouring out life,
that alabaster vial
of costly ointment,
at the feet of One
Who washes others
with His tears.

Prayer is
asking nothing,
desiring nothing
but this,
only this.

                              Bonnie Thurston

When you pray, be like the mountain
   in stillness, in silence;
   thoughts rooted in eternity.
   Do nothing; just sit, just be;
and you will harvest the fruit of your prayer.

When you pray, be like the flower
   reaching up to the sun;
   straight stemmed like a column.
   Be open, ready to accept all things without fear
and you will not lack light on your way.

When you pray, be like the ocean
   with stillness in its depths
   the waves ebbing and flowing
   Have calm in your heart, and evil thoughts
will flee of their own accord.

When you pray, remember the breath
   that made us men living beings,
   from God it comes; to God it returns.
Blend the Word and prayer with the flow of life
and nothing will come between you and the Giver
   of Life.

When you pray, be like the bird,
   endlessly singing before the Creator
   its song rising like incense.
   Pray like the turtle dove
and you will never lose heart.

St Seraphim of Sarov

What a thing it is
to sit absolutely alone,
in the forest at night,
cherished by this wonderful,
unintelligible,
perfectly innocent speech,
the most comforting speech in the world,
the talk that the rain makes by itself all over the
ridges,
and the talk of the watercourses everywhere in the
hollows!
Nobody started it,
nobody is going to stop it.
It will talk as long as it wants, this rain.
As long as it talks
I am going to listen.

Thomas Merton

You do not have to
Look for anything, just
Look.
You do not have to
Listen for specific
Sounds, just
Listen.
You do not have to
Accomplish anything, just
Be.
And in the
Looking, and the
Listening, and the
Being, find
Me.

Ann Lewin

I desire to be all silence,
all adoration,
to penetrate ever deeper and deeper into God,
and to be so filled with God
that I may by my prayer
give him to those who do not know him.

                        Elizabeth of the Trinity

4

Attention

> We are responsible for most of our own blindness and deaf-
> ness. Yet the spirit of God goes on renewing the gift.[1]

Bishop John V. Taylor, who writes as a poet as well as a priest,
faces me with two things: my failure to see and to hear, and the
continuing generosity of God. I cry out like the blind man in the
Gospels, 'Master, I want my sight back', to a Christ who in his
earthly life was always healing men and women and restoring
them to fullness of life and energy. The gift of sight was after all
one of God's earliest gifts to the earthling, the dust-person in the
garden of Eden, and in Genesis we are given that first glimpse of
the sight of beauty: 'every tree that is pleasant to the sight'. Did
Adam and Eve at first enjoy those trees, and see them with wonder
and delight, and did everything change with the desire to possess
the fruit of the tree? Was that when things began to go wrong?
Are we being told about the connection between wonder and
delight and non-attachment – about standing back with reverence
and awe and being aware of the destructive impulse of wanting
to own and to control?

This way of seeing, in other words, is close to mystery, carrying
a sense of what John V. Taylor calls 'the sense of beyondness at
the heart of things'. This is seeing, but seeing beyond. It is seeing
with the eyes of the heart; it is seeing with the inner eye which
recognizes inward beauty; it is seeing with 'rinsed eyes' – eyes
washed clear by contemplation, as was said of both the early

Celtic hermits and of Thomas Merton in his years in his hermitage at Gethsemani. It is a glorious phrase, expressive of the gift of gazing with wonder, with astonishment or amazement, and it is summed up in what Merton said so simply and so frequently:

> Open your eyes and see.

It was something that he returned to frequently, in his writing, his lectures and his poetry, for what he wished above all was that we should learn to 'see directly what is in front of us'.

> It is good and praiseworthy
> to look at some real created thing
> and to feel and appreciate its reality.
> Just let the reality of what is real sink into you.[2]

ᥱᥫᐧᩛᥲ

Time and again the writer, the artist, the poet will remind us that we are living in a transparent world, and that all we have to do is to open our eyes and to see – as they see. Sometimes they jolt us with a shock of surprise which forces us to look anew at something which we had failed to see, whether through over-familiarity, or laziness, or because of the speed with which we habitually live and work.

It is the act of noticing and cherishing which Mary Oliver says makes her a poet. She tells us how she walks and she notices:

> I am sensual in order to be spiritual.
> I look into everything without cutting into
> anything.

She goes for a walk, she trips over a root, a petal, some trivia, and then comes home and says 'It was wonderful!'.[3]

Yet she is only telling us what we all are capable of – which is to see the world as wonder-filled. It may mean opening our eyes to what we had not noticed, and perhaps something that hitherto we had not regarded as worthy of attention. Even so sensitive a man as the potter Michael Cardew tells us in his autobiography that he did not really see until he met his future wife, a painter:

> I failed to *see*, in the way that painters see. I could not see their purple shadows or pink leaves because I looked at the world not with the innocent eyes of a child or a painter but with the prosaic intellectual eyes of one who has been trained to use his head rather than his senses. I did not begin to understand what made Mariel make a drawing of two or three crusts, and a dirty white plate on a table.[4]

Michael Cardew sees because of his wife's eye, Ruth Bidgood learns from watching her artist neighbour:

> [The] girl would sit at the tent-door,
> painting again and again from across the river
> the house at Bryndolau, not beautiful to me
> till seen in her small careful watercolours –
> sunlit brown, grey, green, blue
> laid thick, intense as oil.[5]

Something not apparently beautiful becomes beautiful as one sees afresh. The actual place may not be so important; it does not matter in the end if it is a gentle Welsh hillside or an untidy table. It is the eye which counts. The eye can be entranced by a street scene as much as a scene of natural beauty. The poet, novelist and journalist P. J. Kavanagh has a restless eye, always on the alert, looking out for the unassuming detail. I discovered that he shared my delight in travelling on the top of a London bus:

> I settled myself on the crowded top deck, wiped the window with my sleeve, and prepared to enjoy the flamboyant intricacy of some of the drain pipes on buildings in Sloane Street. I forget who it was who advised me always to look above the shopfronts, and that I would be amazed at the variety of architecture that survives.

But it is not only buildings. Elsewhere he tells us that he was halted by the sight of an advertisement hoarding:

Successive posters had partly peeled off, they were faded, rain-stained, wind-tattered, it was entirely beautiful, and gave the impression of waiting for this to be noticed.[6]

I know how *vital* it is, using that word in its full implication of being life-giving, to live in the present moment, and yet I fail time and again. It is vital because when we become aware and awake to the present moment, we are also awake to God, and then everything can become a moment of miracle, a mysterious reality. For God is only to be found in the reality of this present moment. 'Be a son of this instant' said Thomas Merton in *Raids on the Unspeakable*, after meditating on the Sufi mystic Ibn Abbad – and this is of course the point at which mystics and poets of all traditions, Christian and non-Christian converge.

But how does one enter into that sense of God being there, right before us, loving and acting in the universe at every moment? Merton spoke of what the unique moment meant for him as 'the sense of water on the skin'. The Benedictine vow of stability, by which he lived when he became a Trappist monk in 1941 in Kentucky, helped him here since it gave him the anchor which his earlier wandering and rootless life had lacked. For stability means not only geographical stability of place, but even more profoundly the inner stability of heart and mind, which brings the strength to resist the allurement of turning from the reality of the present by escaping into dreams, fantasies of past or future.

This is something that all those living under the Rule of St Benedict experience, as the Benedictine sister, Sr Macrina Wiederkehr says:

> If I'm slavishly attached to the
> previous moment,
> or if I'm already living tomorrow's moments,
> then I am not free
> for the moment of the eternal now.[7]

Another woman uses the image of a visitation:

> Simple attention to the present moment,
> so that each moment stands alone,
> and becomes a visitation,
> a presence in its own right.

These words come from a book whose title is *Let Evening Come, Reflections on Ageing*,[8] and it is significant that it so often happens that the intensity of vision is heightened at times of extremity, illness or approaching death. Diagnosed with Lou Gehrig's disease while still in his thirties Philip Simmons had to learn the art of falling, of falling gracefully. When he came to write his book *Learning to Fall* (which was published shortly after his death), he said that his illness had also taught him the mastery of falling into every present moment without trying to escape from it. His concern was to be fully present, even when in the midst of pain, and he saw how little of this there is in contemporary American culture. 'The present moment, like the spotted owl or the sea turtle, has become an endangered species.' People would rather deal with abstractions than be awakened out of sleep. With his own impending death before him he thinks about what it means to surrender control, to release the grasping, fearful self in order to enjoy the moment and God's presence within it.[9]

Jean-Pierre de Caussade made the phrase 'the sacrament of the present moment' very familiar, and his words need to be recalled and reclaimed again and again so that over-familiarity does not blunt them. It is good therefore to be told that living in the present moment is an art which requires fostering, as Abraham Joshua Heschel reminds us:

> The art of awareness of God,
> the art of sensing His presence in our daily lives
> cannot be learned off-hand.
> God's grace resounds in our lives
> like a staccato.
> Only by retaining the seemingly disconnected notes
> comes the ability
> to grasp the theme.[10]

Living in the present with total attention is gift given to the artist and the poet, but it can equally well belong to any of us. May Sarton makes us aware of the intensity of the 'staccato note' of each moment as she notes in her journal:

> Afternoon light marbling a white wall
> may take on the quality of revelation.[11]

In a longer passage in her *Journal of a Solitude* she continues this theme of *revelation*:

> If one looks long enough at almost anything,
> looks with absolute attention at a flower,
> a stone,
> the bark of a tree,
> grass, snow, a cloud,
> something like revelation takes place.
> Something is 'given',
> and perhaps that something
> is always a reality *outside* the self.

We can understand when reading this how when she talked about poetry to her students she would quote one of her favourite sayings of Simone Weil, 'Absolute attention is prayer', and would then go on to say:

> I don't know exactly what a prayer is.
> I do know how to pay attention,
> how to fall down into the grass,
> how to kneel down in the grass.[12]

⟨❦⟩

Something like revelation was also true in the case of Philip
Toynbee, struggling with depression and intermittent alcoholism,
who in coming to live in the Forest of Dean in Gloucestershire
was also coming to Christianity. In February 1978 he wrote this
in his journal:

> the basic command of religion
> is not 'do this!'
> or 'do not do that!'
> but simply look!

In his journal, modestly titled *Part of a Journey*, we can follow
him and see how he came to *see*, in a way that he had never done
before. It was due above all to the trees, and it all began one
November day in 1977 when the rain had made gardening impossible and instead he set out for what he called a serious walk,
walking for walking's sake:

> A free and purposeful man!
> And a changed world!
> For on this walk I stopped several times and looked
> at a single tree as I haven't done for years.
> No, I've never done in my life before.
> The tree was there and now, in its own immediate and
> peculiar right; that tree and no other.

Three days later he set out on a much wilder walk and found
that he could now repeat the tree experience almost at will, and
that it was in no way pantheistic:

No feeling that the tree and I are One. Quite the contrary: a sharp awareness of the tree's individual identity. I hope never to lose that vision of the tree's 'inscape': its very potent self and presence.

A few days later this new gift of seeing is moving into loving:

Tree scrutiny ... I stand apart and look; looking I respect, almost to the point of love. But what I hope to be loving is God; not because he 'made' the tree, but because he gives me the power to see it with such intensity and clarity.

His vision is total – he does not select. He enjoys a bare apple tree in the bright wind, seeing how graceless it is, writhing and straining, all elbows. Yet he finds it is as good for scrutiny as the most elegantly sweeping beech, 'for not beauty but *entity* is the thing'.

A professional writer like Philip Toynbee can make us see, help us to see, and a good writer will use all the skills of literary art, as when on one February day he captures for us this sight of the wild geese flying over the nearby Severn Channel:

A wedge of wild geese flying above us and over the Severn sands at Newnham. An ice-clear sky, of the palest violet. Such yearning in those long necks stretched towards the east; and yet such ease and grace in the movement of the wings.

But then he warns, 'But watch that symbol-hunting! Geese are best at being geese.'[13]

He was a writer and a man whose trade lay in the pleasure of handling words, but as he walks and tree-gazes, and he is anxious that his words might generalize the tree, decorate it and yet blur it, he wonders whether a photograph might be rather less offensive.

Thomas Merton was of course a writer and a teacher, and a poet, but he was also a photographer, and it is from his photographs that we learn much about how he saw the world, and how he prayed – and the two are of course intimately connected. He was the son of artist parents and although he has left some pleasing calligraphic line drawings, he never developed his artistic skills in that direction. But he handled a camera as an artist would, and used it as an instrument of delight and perception. It was in the later 1950s that the journalist John Howard Griffin visited Merton in his hermitage. He had his camera with him and when Merton showed an almost childlike fascination he let him keep it on extended loan. At first when Merton sent him the negatives, John Howard Griffin was puzzled, for his view was so different from that of most people. Merton photographed whatever crossed his path – a battered fence, a rundown wooden shack, weeds growing between cracks, working gloves thrown down on a stool, a dead root, a broken stone wall. He approached each thing with attention, he never imposed, he allowed each thing to communicate itself to him in its own terms, and he gave it its own voice.

Later on when he was out in the woods with a young friend, Ron Seitz, both with their cameras, Merton reprimanded him severely for the speed with which he approached things. He told him to stop looking and to begin *seeing*:

> Because looking means that you already have something in mind for your eye to find; you've set out in search of your desired object and have closed off everything else presenting itself along the way. But seeing is being open and receptive to what comes to the eye; your vision total and not targeted.[14]

But he handled people in the same way, a parallel which John Howard Griffin noticed and commented on. He would focus on the other, so thoroughly giving himself to the other that nothing seemed to be held back, and yet left them to be themselves, never seeking to alter, to possess, to improve. He tells us something of this as he describes seeing people in the streets of Louisville on one of his earliest expeditions outside the monastery in 1948:

I found that everything stirred me with a deep and mute sense of compassion. Perhaps some of the people we saw going about the streets were hard and tough – but I did not observe it because I seemed to have lost an eye for merely exterior detail and to have discovered, instead, a deep sense of respect and love.[15]

Here was the sacramental quality of the particular, whether in person or thing, and Merton knew that we have a responsibility to see it, to cherish and to reverence it. He saw how it had been lived out in the lives of the Shakers and in the Shaker community, not so far from the monastery, which he visited and which he wrote about in a book that has long since sadly been out of print, *Religion in Wood*. Here workaday benches, tables, chairs all carried a deep religious character, each thing fulfilling its own vocation, made according to their order and use. The Shaker craftsmen would work patiently, lovingly, earnestly until the work was just right, the fruit of their love and care. Merton found in their furniture a concrete, practical expression of that deep mystery – the way in which a thing may be 'attuned to the music intoned in each being by God the Creator'.

He used his camera primarily as a contemplative instrument. He captured the play of light and dark, the ambience, the inner life. But above all he struggled towards an expression of silence through the visual image, so that his photographs show us that ultimately his concern was to communicate the essence of silence. It was fitting that when after his death John Howard Griffin published some of his photographs – again sadly in a book long out of print – he called it 'A Hidden Wholeness' and gave in the frontispiece this quotation from *Hagia Sophia*:

> There is in all visible things
> an invisible fecundity,
> a dimmed light,
> a hidden wholeness . . .

There is in all things
an inexhaustible sweetness and purity,
a silence that is a fountain of action and of joy.
It rises up in wordless gentleness
and flows out to me
from the unseen roots of all created being.[16]

I have gained much from the notebooks and journals of writers, poets, artists for here I am given the raw material, as it were of their work, their immediate response to the apparently small and insignificant trivia of daily life. The American writer Anne Lamott tells us something very significant about the art of writing when she says, 'I think that in order to be a writer you have to learn to be reverent'. She uses the phrase 'compassionate detachment', and explains that while there should be a certain distancing, it is not the distancing of a detachment which does not care, but rather the standing apart, the non-possession, that comes out of caring, a deep, almost passionate caring.[17]

The discipline of keeping a journal, and not least for a short space of time, can in fact become one of the most useful instruments of awareness, attentiveness for any of us. In a most extraordinary way it can become an experience that makes one feel more fully alive, more attentive, more conscious of and connected to the world around, whatever shape or form those surroundings might take. So perhaps keeping a notebook, a journal, might also play a creative part in this time of retreat?

Walking in Awareness

I begin in silence and as I start to enter that silence I try to become aware of my breathing. I spend a moment or two to alert myself to God's presence, and to take a deep breath of air. With gratitude I thank God for this air which I can so easily take for granted, and yet it is the substance of my life, of all life, it comes from that unceasing generosity of God which holds me and the whole universe in existence.

I start to walk very slowly and deliberately. As I place my feet (and if it is possible and sensible I am barefoot) on the ground I try to be aware that I am blessed by it and in turn I bless it. This is a reciprocal act of giving and receiving.

> O God to bless the earth beneath my feet;
> O God let the earth bless me.

I want to use all my senses, the fullness of my physical self, and at the point I list those five God-given gifts: of sight, touch, hearing, taste, smell.

I try to stop thinking and instead simply to be.

I try to let go, to let everything drop away so that I can be totally present to whatever may reach me through my senses.

My first act is to listen, and if I stand still, with closed eyes, it helps to sharpen my perception of the variety of sounds around me – sounds close to me, nearer sounds and distant sounds, the sounds that come from the earth and those that come from the sky.

If I am somewhere in a city there will probably be only the sounds made by human activity. Yet even here we should listen with openness, for as a New York apartment dweller, bound by his agoraphobic condition to remain indoors, can say, 'sounds

move you emotionally', as he learnt to listen to the sounds from
the streets below.

Even if I manage to find what seems like silence then even that
apparent silence is in fact teeming with sound – as we are
reminded in the story of Elijah when he finds himself surrounded
by what a modern translation renders as a 'sound of sheer silence'
(1 Kings. 19.12).

When I open my eyes and I begin to walk, I do so slowly and
deliberately. I want to look with both the outer and the inner
eye, taking in a wide arc from the height of the heavens to the
ground below me. I begin to notice the diversity of structures,
shapes outlined against the sky, patterns in all their diversity, light
and shadow, in their contrasts, and the relationships between
them. As my vision sharpens I begin to see the range of the colour
green in the country. It may be that I find something that is only
a part, a fragment of the whole, yet it is still to be treasured, for
each unique element has a worth of its own.

In the town I may have to make more of an effort if I am
walking the streets I know well with a new eye. I begin with my
feet, looking at the cracks in the pavements, the variety of pattern
of the drain-covers, or the gas mains, and then I look upwards
to the roof level, to the clusters of chimney pots in all their variety
of design set against the sky, or the starkness of the silhouettes
of the television masts and aerials with their dramatic geometric
shapes.

Before I begin to use my hands to touch anything, I first
consciously try to feel how I myself am being touched by air,
sun, wind, on my skin, and then I try to become aware of the
pull of gravity through the pressure of the ground under my feet
and how that brings me balance. I feel the tensed muscles of a
tree or the stress within a rock. And then I start to touch as many
things as I can, picking them up and feeling their texture, enjoying
their tactile quality. Even the stems and stalks of the most
common of grasses and wild flowers show such amazing diversity:
square or round, smooth, hairy, tough, hollow . . . Then I turn

to pebbles, small stones, scraps of twig and branch, fir-cones or conkers or whatever may be in season. As I hold them in the palm of my hand and let their weight and shape make themselves known to me, I ponder their mystery, remembering that the word ponder has its root in *pondus*, weight. I touch things gently with fingers and finger-tips, for it takes time to appreciate the differing textures, and to realize how many such things there are waiting for me to relate to them.

What a miracle of ingenuity there is here, and how often I tend to pass it by in my usual rushing life.

The smell of town and country changes with the seasons. With the sun comes a strong, heady smell, the winter brings a sharper edge. The sense of smell, the strongest sense in the animal world, is one for human beings most frequently associated with the consumer world of expensive scents and cosmetics or deodorants and after-shave. Yet we are surrounded by natural scents, the range of natural smells waiting for us when we take time to rub leaves or crush stalks.

Taste will be the most challenging of the senses to nourish as I walk. But I can at least chew a blade of grass or find an edible leaf.

As well as focusing on one single thing I must also try to let my eyes sweep over the whole horizon with unfocused attention and delight in the riches and profusion of the totality of the scene.

> Here is exuberance and extravagance
> profusion of colour
> cacophony of sound
> abundance.

Finally, if I were to repeat this walk, perhaps make it a daily part of the time of retreat, I will almost certainly discover that by revisiting a place I find more there than I saw at first, and this in itself tells me something about the art of looking, seeing, gazing.

Prayers and Reflections

Dear God, are you the Friend I can trust?

. . .

let me pause and remember
the holy ground of your presence –
the bush burning with light . . .

You are here in the ones I ignore;
the shuffling old man in the street,
the hollow-eyed woman unkempt,
the neighbour I pass hurriedly by.

. . .

I see neither their need nor mine,
it is I who turn silent away.
. . . No wonder I do not hear your voice
I turn away from your presence.

Psalm 28

Wonder at things that are before thee,
making this the first step to further knowledge.

Clement of Alexandria

This is the enchantment, this is the exuberance,
the all-compensating wonder.
Giving to common things wild kindred
with the gold-tesserate floors of Joye.

Francis Thompson, 'An Anthem of Earth'

The farthest star and the mud at my feet are a family; and there is no decency or sense in honoring one thing, or a few things, and then closing the list.

Mary Oliver

Over the swinging parapet of my arm
your sentinel eyes lean gazing. Hugely alert
in the pale unfinished clay of your infant face,
they drink light from this candle on the tree.
Drinking, not pondering, each bright thing you see,
you make it yours without analysis
and, stopping down the aperture of thought
to a fine pinhole, you are filled with flame.

Give me for Christmas, then, your kind of seeing,
not studying candles – angel, manger, star –
but staring as at a portrait, God's I guess,
that shocks and holds the eye, till all my being,
gathered, intent and still, as now you are,
breathes out its wonder in a wordless yes.

John V. Taylor

It is by your Lov
that you enjoy all His Delights,
and are Delightfull to Him.

Thomas Traherne

People think pleasing God is all God cares about. But any fool in the world can see he is always trying to please us back.

Alice Walker *The Color Purple*

You are the awakening
you await by the roadside
but do not know,
cannot see,
the eyes of your heart
being darkened,
blinded
by tinsel and neon
to the star
which has risen
in the east
and points the way
toward dawn.

Visible
across the vast
expanse of eternity,
you can glimpse it
even here.
But you must close
your inner eye
to this world's
false twinkling,
and step outside
your little self
into the shining darkness
of world without end.

Bonnie Thurston

On the day of Judgement God will only ask one question:
Did you enjoy my world?

Traditional Jewish saying

Though the limit of our life is short,
praise can lengthen it,
for, corresponding to the extent of our love,
we shall acquire, through praise, life that has no
                                    measure,

O Lord, may my body be a temple for him who built it,
may the soul be a palace full of praise for its
                                    architect.

                                    Ephrem

5

Change

Michelangelo, engaged in sculpting one of his statues, is reputed to have said: 'Another few days and life will break through.' If I am taking this as my starting point on this day of the retreat it is because these words from an artist make me see myself as raw material, open to being shaped and fashioned, open to new life. Yet when I watch the process by which stone becomes a statue, I am made aware of just how slow and how costly it has to be, and how undramatic. In recent years by visiting the stonemasons' yard of my local cathedral I have been able to watch decayed stones of a great medieval building being replaced and renewed by new stones straight from the quarry. It is often difficult to see much progress, and the skill of the craftsmen shows me just how laborious and yet simultaneously how delicate their work must be. It is a strange art, for it starts with what is an immense block of clumsy, raw, unshaped stone, which by being simplified and shaped is changed into something new. This gives me an image to help me on this day of the retreat when I want to reflect on change on my journey towards God, and the costliness of being shaped, transformed.

When I visited an exhibition in London, entitled 'The Image of Christ', one sculpture immediately caught my attention. It was called 'Christ on the Cold Stone', a late medieval work which shows the naked Christ, wearing only a crown of thorns, sitting on a rock awaiting crucifixion. I realized that this is never mentioned in the gospels, and rarely spoken of. Yet this anonymous artist made me aware of how this must have been a time when Christ was at his most vulnerable. The statue has caught a posture of physical and spiritual anguish, which portrays the depths of suffering, indeed of inconsolable sorrow.

> O all ye that pass by the way,
>   attend,
> and see if there be any sorrow
>   like to my sorrow.

(Lamentations 1.12)

It was profoundly moving to stand before this scene of Christ's humanity; it is as though he knows and carries the whole human condition. The fact that he sits on bare rock is a reminder that soon this body, born in a stone feeding trough (rather than a manger or crib of the romantic imagination) will be laid to rest in a stone tomb. We know of course that this is not the end of the story, that the tomb will open and that the pain and suffering will lead to the resurrection and new life.[1]

The feet that are now resting on the ground in an attitude of total weariness will soon be immobilized by the nails of the cross. This is the prelude to inconceivable darkness, pain, suffering. But the theme of this day of the retreat is that of transformation and transfiguration, the paschal mystery in which the darkness, pain and suffering are transformed into resurrection and new life. This is the goal and end of the journey. But for most of us the experience of the journey itself will not be one of continual, ongoing progress. Although we yearn for the light and long to go 'into the world of light', we find instead that the pattern of our human life means living between both dark and light in a process that is never simple.

A poet has the courage to write on what times of darkness can mean:

Unlike Eurydice
most of us
do not just descend
to the Underworld.
We carry it with us,
a dark place,
many dark places.

Even on clear days
it casts shadows,
threatens to swallow
present sweetness
as it has past.

But she is also a gardener and elsewhere she writes this:

I am a gardener, I know
plants grow at the bottom first,
root before stem,
stem before flower.
The soil must be rich, dark, I must water until it's
                                                    soaked

so thirsty roots
will go deep to drink
not fan out on the surface
to wither in the heat, . . .

go down first,
trust depths and darkness,
then flower.[2]

It is hardly surprising that the journey theme should be among
the great archetypes of world literature, for while the journey
that we all make is totally unique, it is also something which
we all share. The myths and legends of the odyssey, the search

for the holy grail, the quest for the isles of the blessed, are timeless. Abraham set out not knowing where he was going and that is a story which is told and re-told time and again, not least because the desert setting is an image which touches us all; the word itself significantly in Hebrew meaning a place that is unexplored and unsurveyed. Here is stark emptiness in which horizon after horizon opens up. This was the setting for Abraham's journey:

a journeying existence, from dawn to sunset, his eyes always on the horizon. He wasn't very well equipped; he went out not knowing whither he went; but however merciless the journey, through rain, sandstorm, wind and the heart of the desert sun, on he went, thinking of the city that hath the foundations, whose builder and maker is God. That was his horizon – God's place for him. But when Abraham reached the horizon on his long journey he would there and then find another horizon in the far distance, calling to him, and on he would go again. Horizons must continually be reached and lost ... Tents must be pitched for a night and struck when the light of a new dawn appears ... We must travel light if we want to keep pace with Christ.[3]

If we are to follow Christ on the journey we find a man whose earthly life held no security. In an article that George McCleod wrote for the journal which he called *The Coracle* and which was issued by the Iona community in its early years, this appeared in June 1942:

Jesus was always on the move. 'I must walk today, tomorrow and the next day' was the motto of his ministry. He went before them and they were amazed, and as they followed they were afraid ... He assured his disciples down the centuries that 'He had many things to tell them but they could not bear them ... but when the Spirit of truth was come he would guide them into all truth', i.e. the fuller and fuller truth would be revealed as they move.

And then comes his picture of Jesus, told with all the vigour and immediacy that we have come to associate with this great prophetic figure as he tried in his own life and ministry to follow the fearless figure of St Columba:

> we find that he was content to be born as a gypsy in a shelter by the roadside; to minister with no place to lay his head; and to die, at a crossroads where three civilizations gathered. Even as he find that the first word he had for all his followers was not to read, or even to pray, but to GO.[4]

It is fascinating to find that it was the coracle which George McLeod should choose as the image to express his venture on Iona, for among the many journey themes none has captured the imagination more vividly than the Celtic *peregrini*. These wandering saints of the early Celtic period set out in their coracles, fragile craft of hides stretched over a wooden frame, without oars, to go wherever the spirit might take them. They knew only that the goal and end of their voyaging was to come to the place of their resurrection. We too must travel light, in every sense of that word, if we wish to travel with the man who had nowhere to lay his head and who said to his followers 'Come, follow me' – to wherever that might lead. Few people have taken this as literally as did those wandering saints of the early Celtic period, fearless monks, on fire with the love of Christ. The geographical circumstances and the external conditions were not in the end so important, for this came from an inner prompting, an inner conviction. This is an inward journey for love, the love of Christ. If Christ is the end of the journey he is equally the impulse towards the journey, the support on the journey.

> Pilgrimage is a journeying toward God. It expresses the yearning of the heart to be in the presence of God; during

pilgrimage the self is pointed toward the destination. It is a
physical embodiment of inclining the heart toward God.

These words come from *The God we Never Knew*[5] by the popular American theologian Marcus Borg, and although I appreciate
his words, they remain abstract and leave me with questions:
Where and how shall I begin? What equipment do I need? Is
there guidance for the journey?

I do not want a scientific atlas but something more like a sketch
map from travellers who have gone before me and who can chart
the route because they have themselves traversed it. St Benedict,
that most down-to-earth of spiritual guides writes, as do all monastics, out of hard-won human experience. But he does have his
mystical side which comes across most forcibly in those verses in
the Prologue to the Rule where he is addressing his disciples, and
indeed all of us, and encouraging us to embark on the journey
that will bring us to Christ. We have already seen how he speaks
of the astonished eye and the thunderstruck ear, a reference to
the drowsy disciples and their being roused by the shining forth
of Christ at the Transfiguration. So we see the further image –
one that is central to our exploration today – when he uses the
words *deificum lumen*, 'the light that comes from God', or more
accurately, the light that makes us like God, or shapes us into
the likeness of God.

We are to be changed. Unless we believe that, is there any
point in our lives? We cannot change other people, one of the
hardest lessons of all, but we can change ourselves. Everything in
the Rule, as in the gospel, points to the risen Christ, to the paschal
mystery, to the mystery of death and new life. Just as sight and
hearing are to be open and not closed up, so also is that true of
the heart. St Benedict does not want us to go through life with
a shut up heart; nor does he want us to become half-hearted. He
refuses to patronize us with any assurance that things will be easy
or even that they will get better in the future. The road may still
be difficult and the way ahead demanding, but he does promise

that there will be *change* and the change will come in us. This is the promise: *dilatato corde inerrabili dilectionis dulcedine*, which in the Latin reads so beautifully with this deliberate alliteration that gets lost in translation and which gives the sense of a love that is pure delight. Our hearts will grow, expand, swell . . . The words themselves may vary, the picture remains the same, God at work in us enlarging our hearts until they are 'overflowing with the inexpressible delight of love' – the ineffable love of 1 Corinthians 2.9.

When I read this in conjunction with a passage in St John Chrysostom where he is writing of how heat will make things expand, I find that this becomes a very powerful image:

> Just as what brings heat makes things expand
> so it is the gift of love
> to stretch hearts wide open; it is a warm and
> glowing virtue.

He then goes on to write of how love caused St Paul to open his heart of love and to embrace all:

> And yet his love did not stretch to breaking point,
> nor become weak,
> but remained whole in every case.[6]

To enlarge means to increase in capacity, with the implication that the vessel becomes more open and receptive, waiting to be filled. The divine potter is shaping the raw clay of my being, is making me into a larger and larger vessel. I co-operate by being willing and not resistant, for essentially this is God at work on me. Being shaped by God means living open to grace, to 'the inspiration and energy of grace'. I am in the hands of a God who can do all things, as St Benedict puts it, *Dominus qui omnia potest operare salutem* (28.5), though I must not imagine that he is going to 'do all things' in the way that I might expect. My journey is a matter of being acted upon by God as Michael Casey reminds us:

The primary cause of progress is being willing to receive this gift and to be willing at the same time to remove from our hearts and lives anything that inhibits this receptivity.[7]

As monastics have always known, the most powerful factor at work upon us, acting to make change, transformation, possible, is the Word of God. So once again I turn to mentors who give me encouragement and practical help. The *opus Dei*, the work of God, the gathering to share in the hearing of the Word and the singing of the psalms, was central to the monastic *horarium*, the daily timetable, and St Benedict says that God is present in a unique way in these regular times of common, shared prayer:

> We believe that God is present everywhere and that the eyes of the Lord gaze everywhere on the good and on the bad (Prov. 15.3). We should though be totally convinced that this is so when we are present at the divine office.

When we learn that in his day the canticles and psalms would be chanted by a soloist cantor and the choir of monks would respond with a refrain, we appreciate the significance of what he says about paying attention:

> And so we should always recall at such times the words of the psalms 'serve the Lord with awe and reverence', and sing the Lord's praises with skill and relish ... That will lead us to make sure that, when we sing in choir, there is complete harmony between the thoughts in our mind and the meaning of the words we sing.[8]

This harmony of mind and voice applies equally to my own self for it is again about attitude, the priority of the interior over what is external. St Benedict discusses it in chapter 19 and when the Cistercian, Michael Casey was lecturing on this chapter to Australian apostolic Benedictines, the Good Samaritan Sisters, he made comments that I have taken the liberty of changing into the personal so that what he was saying about the formative and transformative power of the Scriptures might read in the form of a reflection which I can apply to myself:

> In this way I shall be shaped
> in my whole inner being,
> according to the inspired words of
>   the text that I am saying,
> I am possessed by God's Word;
> it enters into composition with my own
>   subjectivity
> and acts as leaven
> in the process of my transformation.[9]

Transformation comes about when we are willing to admit God's word into our lives, to hear God's voice and to act upon it. Mind, senses, heart, must all be open to receive. This means that we must pay attention without being passive – listening, hearing, reflecting. At this point the monastic understanding of humility has a role to play. It is unfortunate that it is a concept which has become so unattractive, and carries associations of low self-esteem, for in fact its true meaning lies in the proper sense of self. It means knowing and accepting my limitations, and not denying them; I am not in charge; I am not the ultimate source of wisdom. I am not self-sufficient; I cannot manage on my own. When I admit that God is in charge I am willing and ready to change, probably time and time again – which is simply another way of saying that I am ready to open myself up to a process of continuing transformation. St Benedict gave his monks a triad of silence, obedience and humility as the basic tools for their vocation. Taken together they enrich one another. Translated into my own circumstances I see them as asking of me the triad of silence, listening, emptiness, and the commitment to being a disciple, *discipulus*, one who learns, who follows, who is ready to open up to the new.

The way of living which St Benedict wished for his disciples is no different from that which any of us today might follow if we want to live life fully and freely. His concern was not only for the opened eyes and ears that I discussed earlier, but equally important, for a heart and mind that are also open. And if this way of openness is risky, that is no more than his concern to prevent the stifling of that freedom which a closed mind brings. When we live in a world which seems to be becoming increasingly polarized, and where fundamentalism, whether in religion or in politics, seems to attract so many people with its offer of certainty, the Benedictine tradition offers us something counter-cultural. It is most clearly set out in the final chapter, the epilogue to the Rule, where St Benedict tells his followers that they must read further and where he clearly wants them to take their thinking beyond what they will find in his own writing. He cites on the one hand the Desert Fathers and Cassian, and on the other Basil and Pachomius, thus presenting us with two contrasting traditions – the former emphasizing eremitical and ascetic values, the latter coenobetic, or life of an extended monastic family under a father or mother. He was looking for followers who would be open to different streams of thought; he was telling them to set up a dialectic so that different streams might interact, challenge and stimulate one another. The implications apply to any of us. He is asking us, in the words of Thomas Keating, an American Cistercian monk, for 'mutual respect and full acceptance of one another's orientation'. To live in this way, not only in society and in the Church today, but also more importantly in my own interior self, means recognizing and affirming the riches of diversity and finding in them a source of growth and progress.[10]

In our own day Thomas Merton is the supreme example of a man living a monastic life who always remained open to new and different orientations, willing to draw on widely disparate sources, continually asking fresh questions, exploring new territories of the mind, and breaking boundaries to open up further vistas of his internal geography. Rowan Williams called a lecture that he gave on Merton 'New Words for God', speaking of him being both a poet and a contemplative 'living under a very broad sky, which is sometimes a night sky', a man who resisted all the alluring temptations 'to build shelters or dig holes, even to draw helpful charts of the sky which would allow you to find your way around'. I like these images since if I apply them to myself in this time of retreat they bring me back once again to the themes of a risky and costly openness, and the reminder, in the words with which Rowan Williams ended his lecture, 'of how very easily we become prisoners ... and how very bad prison is for any of us'.[11]

∙∙∙∙∙

Merton was open and ready to learn from so many sources, not only from the great men and women of the past but also from his contemporaries of whatever religious persuasion, or none. The friends and companions whom he met at different points along the way all played their part in enlarging his vision, opening up vistas, forcing him to grow and change. But he was above all moulded by the daily Offices, by the reading and studying of the Scriptures, both in choir with the community and on his own, and most particularly, by his great love of the psalms. Here Merton found bread for the journey just as 500 years before another Cistercian, Aelred the abbot of Rievaulx, had told his Yorkshire community that it was here that they would find 'the saving food of God's word', 'the bread of your pilgrimage'. So we return again to the importance of the Word as the agent of transformation and the support that we shall gain from it when we give it a central place on our journey:

This is *the bread that came down from heaven and gives life to the world.* (John 6.33)

You ask for this bread
just like the children of the Lord Jesus.
By coming here you wish to be fed
especially with the bread that fills the mind
more than the stomach
lest you fall behind on the road (cf. Matt. 15.32).[12]

When Thomas Merton met the Dalai Lama in India in 1968 and was questioned by him about what he felt was fundamental to his Christian monastic life, he spoke of *transformation* as a total and lifelong process:

commitment to total inner transformation of one sort of another – a commitment to become a completely new man. It seems to me that that could be regarded as the end of the monastic life, and that no matter where one attempts to do this, that remains the essential thing.[13]

But earlier in that same year not knowing of course that he was making the final journey of his life, since he was travelling to a conference in Bangkok where he was to die accidentally, he wrote this in his notebook:

> Our real journey in life is interior;
> it is a matter of growth,
> deepening,
> and of an even greater surrender
> to the creative action
> of love and grace in our hearts.

He insisted that while there was a need for effort, deepening, and transformation it was most important not to undertake any special project of self-transformation or some attempt to 'work on myself', but rather

> just go for walks,
> live in peace,
> let change come quietly and invisibly on the
> inside.[14]

ᏇᏕᏸᏕᎤ

I find it consoling when Merton says this – that we should let change come quietly, invisibly, secretly. In my experience change is not only slow, it can also be partial, disappointing, often taking place in the deepest recesses of myself, unnoticed, even imperceptible. And there are times of failure when I do not even seem to move forward at all but slip back. It is good then to remind myself that it may not be until years later that I recognize what was happening and begin to see the underlying pattern of growth.

Yet without the hope of change, life is meaningless, perhaps unlivable. Sometimes, however, sermons and religious writing appear to give the impression that growth and change (particularly when reference is made to the beauty of 'pruning', which I have found a favourite theme of many preachers and authors) is somehow more simple and good than harsh reality suggests. Here story-telling, with the images that it brings, helps to show me just how many patterns of change there are; and I then remind myself that my way is unique to me and that I must resist the dangerous temptation of comparing myself to others, which inevitably makes me feel anxious and competitive. That is why I am grateful for the journals of Philip Toynbee who approaches questions that we all must face with such a refreshing honesty. At one point he re-tells the story of a Sufi saint from which he draws strength:

> There are some who ride on white chargers and leap over the moon. There are others who plod along a muddy road on their own two feet, often slipping back in a day as far as they have advanced in the past month. But both sorts of traveller arrive at the same place in the end.

And then he goes on to reflect that 'the same place' only means that each of us gets as far as we can, this furthest possible point which is unique, for each is unique. And then, using the image of light rather differently from the meaning that it had for St Benedict, he says:

> The beauty of it is that since every human soul is unique the light that it sees and the light that it shines have never been seen or shone before.[15]

For Philip Toynbee the journey into God was a matter of *seepage*, slow seepage, an advancing tide, not some sudden event with a climactic point in which he could claim that before this there was No God and after it, God. God enters gradually, bringing light and meaning to the emerging human mind.[16] This speaks of something that is slow, hidden, mysterious, not always recognized at the time but later on, looking back, can be seen as the result of moments of grace. This is how Merton understood his own early years as he tells us in the *The Seven Storey Mountain*, how he was finally brought to Gethsemani and to his monastic vocation – and to a future of which he imagined God saying, 'I will lead you by the way that you cannot possibly understand'. After five years in the monastery, when he came to write *The Sign of Jonas*, he took the story of Jonah travelling inside the whale in what appeared to be the totally wrong direction as an image of how he had come to see himself, travelling towards his destiny in the belly of a paradox. It was a book, as he explained in his introduction that should be seen 'in this context of ambivalence, of questioning, of supreme spiritual risk'.[17]

To follow a God who moves and who expects us to move with him is a risky undertaking. It means not playing safe, and it asks for confidence in God's hidden purposes. In the wilderness at Massah the people of Israel berated the God whom they felt had abandoned them and let them down; they grumbled and tested him as they demanded, 'Is God amongst us or not?' It is difficult not to feel sympathy for them, for how often when things are going badly have we not asked precisely the same question: Where is God in all of this? That scene in the desert was daily recalled in a Benedictine community who would sing Psalm 94 (95) as part of the first Office of the day – as it was also included in the Anglican service of Mattins since Thomas Cranmer when compiling the *Book of Common Prayer* followed this monastic practice. So down the ages there has been this daily reminder of how easily we fail to trust in God, fail to see the hand of God at work and instead we protest and grumble. I so often find myself asking

'Is God in this or not?'
Can I find God in this apparently unlikely place?
Is God here in these frightening circumstances?
How can I find him in situations of loss, betrayal,
                                          depression?
Is he here in times of disappointment and uncertainty?

I learnt a very simple lesson from my experience of walking the labyrinth in Chartres Cathedral. Sometimes I seemed to be making progress and the next moment I found that I was doubling back on myself, retracing my steps, apparently wasting time and getting nowhere. Although I could always see the centre, I often could not believe that I was actually ever going to reach it. There was therefore only one reality and that was to keep on moving, placing my bare feet on the cold floor and trying to overcome the moments of doubt and panic. I thought of how in ancient mythology there was a monster lurking at the centre, a creature of fear and threat, but now I was making my way to Christ, and the centre no longer stood for fear but for the dissolving of fear. The message of the labyrinth for me was very simply that I must walk in faith, believing that I would ultimately come home. I must not give up; I have to keep going, even when there seems to be no other reality than the demands of putting one foot after another.

The commitment, and often the courage, that is needed to place one foot after another each of us knows in our own peculiar circumstances. There might appear to be a vast distance in time

and place between those earliest Celtic pilgrim monks putting out
to sea in their frail coracles in the sixth or seventh century and
Catherine de Hueck Doherty walking the streets of Harlem, in
twentieth-century New York. Yet they both tell us, in their own
very distinctive terms, that without the sense of the support and
presence of Christ the journey is impossible. The *peregrini* were
clear that it was because they already held Christ in their hearts
that they could set out on their journey to find him. And the
same was true of Catherine. She said that the key to her searching
and longing, which the mercy of God will hand her, was Christ.
As she lived her extraordinary life in those teeming and hostile
streets she said, 'All the time I walked on pavements the soles of
my feet were bloody.' Watching the faces of others, she realized
just how deep the human heart was, involving such a precipitate
and painful descent:

> You walk the journey inward all your life to meet the God
> who dwells within. Going inward may be a precipitate descent
> because hearts are deep . . . It's not just to go into my own
> heart, but also into the hearts of others as well to meet the
> God who dwells there. And if you enter into the hearts of
> others they may well be stony, fragmented stones, not easy
> to walk on, and so again the feet become bloody.[18]

If we are to see the journey as one that takes us downward and
inward, down to all the hardest realities of our lives, we have the
consolation of knowing that Christ is alongside us, a man who
in his own life experienced those harsh realities himself. Van
Gogh's painting came out of his own often unspeakable suffering
yet time and again he painted the wheatfields which were his
prototypical symbol of the cycle of death and rebirth. The intense
blue of those vast turbulent skies, which are such a dominant
feature, are a symbol of the infinite, of the divine presence of

God. He used yellow as the representation of the resurrection. Wheat speaks of the cycle of sowing and harvesting, and of life, birth and rebirth, so in the wheatfield we have a sign of hope. But it is the roads that weave their way through the wheat which are the dominant element, whose vibrant colouring draws our eyes magnetically to them. Sometimes they run out of the picture, sometimes they diverge or disappear into the wheat. They are for Van Gogh the journey of life.

The one extant sermon that we have from his early years within the Dutch church are the words of a young man already aware of the balance between rejoicing and sorrow:

> Our life is a pilgrim's progress . . .
> sorrowful yet always rejoicing,
> rejoicing because it is so far off
> and the road so long;
> hopeful as he looks up to the eternal city far
> away,
> resplendent in the evening glow.
> And he thinks of the old saying
> Much strife must be striven,
> much suffering must be suffered,
> much prayer must be prayed,
> and then the end will be peace.

He produced no less than thirty paintings of sowers, reapers, wheatfields, and they all allude to his notion of journeying. Towards the end of his life the appearance of crows over the wheatfield hints at the darkness which hung over him and was ultimately to lead to his suicide. Yet even in the time of greatest suffering he was able to write this, dated July 1889:

> Learning to suffer without complaint,
> learning to look on pain without repugnance –
> you may even catch a glimpse
> that on the other side of life

we shall see good reason for the existence of pain,
which seen from here
sometimes so fills the horizon
that it takes on the proportion of a hopeless
deluge.
We know very little about this,
about its proportions,
and it is better to look at a wheatfield,
even in the form of a picture.[19]

This day began with the figure of the vulnerable, human, suffering, Christ, the Christ of the cold stone. Later on we shall be thinking about how the crucified Christ is also the victorious and risen Christ. If we are to make the journey of our lives with a sense of his presence with us we should try to hold onto the promise that in the end good will triumph over evil and light over darkness. For this Christ mysteriously present at every step of the way is not only the Way, but also the Truth and the Life. These are three interconnected realities. He is the way because he teaches the truth, and that truth will lead to life.[20]

Prayers and Reflections

Dear God, you sustain and feed me:
like a shepherd you guide me.
You lead me to a oasis of green,
to lie down by restful waters.

Even when cliffs loom out of the mist,
my step is steady because of my trust.
Even when I go through the deepest valley,
I will fear no evil or harm.
For you are with me to give me strength,
your crook, your staff, at my side.

Psalm 23

We did not make ourselves,
it was the Lord who made us,
and it is the Lord, too,
who has remade us,
setting himself from the start
to accomplish the mystery of our salvation ...
the hidden plan who him alone would redeem us –
his mysterious design

. . .

To appreciate so sublime a plan,
so great a gift,
we need his own light to dawn on us from the
                              everlasting hills.

It is to those hills
that we must lift up our eyes
to see how we were saved
from hurtling down the path we now climb.

From a letter by St Paulinus of Nola

He was seventy-five years old
and God's first word to him
was 'Go.'

I think of Abram
when my plans go awry,
when happenstance

pries my fingers loose
from the grasping illusion
of control over life.

'Go,' God said to Abram,
giving no address,
disclosing no destination.

Taking an unruly family,
trusting God to show the way,
Abram went.

On that wild journey
he, too, had fingers pried loose,
heard Sarai laugh, learned

the blessing comes
in the going
and the letting go.

Bonnie Thurston

No need to wonder what heron-haunted lake
   lay in the other valley,
or regret the songs in the forest
I chose not to traverse.
No need to ask where other roads might have led,
since they led elsewhere;
for nowhere but this here and now
is my true destination.
The river is gentle in the soft evening,
and all the steps of my life have brought me home.

Ruth Bidgood

Do you, then, Lord,
rise up to meet me
as I run to meet you.
Since I have not the strength to scale your summits
unless you stretch out your right hand to me
whom your hands have made,
rise to meet me . . .
and *lead me in the way of eternity*,
that is, in Christ,
who is the way by which we journey,
and the eternity which is our journey's end.

Blessed Guerric of Igny, *Sermon*

Friend, I have lost the way.
The way leads on.
Is there another way?
The way is one.
I must retrace the track.
It's lost and gone.

Back, I must travel back!
None goes there, none.
Then I'll make here my place.
(The road runs on),
Stand still and set my face.
(The road leaps on),
Stay here, for ever stay.
None stays here, none.
I cannot find the way.
The way leads on.
Oh places I have passed!
That journey's done.
And what will come at last?
The road leads on.

Edwin Muir

New things are possible for us in our life
once we acknowledge the inner mess,
Jesus comes to life here and now.
And if we begin by saying:
'Where we are, he's been',
we begin to hear the other side of this great message:
'Where he is, we shall be'.

Rowan Williams

And so, after she has risen the Word again says
'Rise'
and after she has come he says 'Come'.
One who has thus risen never lacks the opportunity to
rise further
and one who is running towards the Lord
never reaches the end of the space

available for the divine race.
We should always be rising
and those whom the race is bringing close to the goal
should never stop.
Each time the Word says 'Rise' and 'Come',
he gives the power to ascend to still loftier
                              heights.

St Gregory of Nyssa

6

Dark and Light

They go out, they go out, full of tears,
carrying seed for the sowing:
they come back, they come back, full of song,
carrying their sheaves.

These words of the psalmist tell me, that like the Israelites of old, I go out weeping, carrying the seed, but the promise is that I will return with the joy of harvest.[1] When he writes about the returning exiles the psalmist is referring to the traditional custom of ritual weeping during the sowing of the seed, tears shed for the hidden divinity in the wheat, which must fall to the ground and die and lie there in darkness before it can come to life and fruition.

There is something ageless, elemental in this image of sowing and reaping, on which after all the whole of life depends. The seed is to lie in darkness, in ground that has been carefully but painfully prepared, harrowed and sliced, so that that small grain may enter into the hidden depths and remain there until it emerges to face the stranglehold of weeds and other hazards. But finally, drawn by the light and warmth of the sun, it will come to fulfilment and fruition at the time of harvest. There are four elements which must play their part in all human experience, earth, fire, water, air. Sometimes they are put in the form of a circle, with fire placed on the outside and earth at the centre, and in between come water and air binding them together. Life is not possible without water.

It is difficult to see through eyes blinded by weeping. And yet the psalmist tells us that tears and joy belong together and make one another fruitful. The darkness of the womb of the earth and the rays of the sun work together to bring life. Here again is a duality that is both mystery and mercy. So my reading and my praying today will take me into the exploration of the inter-connectedness and the mutual inter-dependency of dark and light. This may well mean that I have to confront things in my own life that are hidden, or pain-filled. Yet it is only by bringing them out into the light, watering them with tears that, just like the seed buried in the depths of the earth, they will become life-giving, and like the harvest, a blessing to myself and to others.

The time of darkness may well be one of loneliness, of doubt and anguish. On the day before Christmas Eve 1979, Fr Christian, the French Trappist abbot was 1,000 miles south of his monastery Tibhirine, in what is known as the Sinai of Algiers. It was an isolated plateau of windswept cliffs and rocks where once Charles de Foucauld had built a small stone hut in which to spend time in solitude. In this barren mountain of granite rocks he wrote these words:

> Nuits de la foie en agonie . . .
> Le doute est la, et la folie
> d'aimer tout seul un Dieu absent et captivant.
> . . . Ce que j'espere, je ne le vois . . .
> C'est mon tourment, tourne vers lui.
> Toute souffrance y prend son sens,
> cache en Dieu comme une naissance,
> ma JOIE deja, mais c'est la NUIT.[2]

The monastery's journal recorded that he returned smiling, unshaven, emaciated. Fr Christian was now sure of his monastic vocation, counting on the transforming power of prayer to have 'the courage and patience to place hope in the accomplishment of small things, each and every day'. There is in his experience something that crosses all the boundaries of time and place. When the Irish poet Seamus Heaney visited one of those small Celtic bothies or beehive huts which are to be found on the headlands of the west coast of Ireland he tells how those sixth- or seventh-century solitaries knew both the darkness of the stone and the dazzle of the light outside and how they moved from one to the other. Because he writes in prose that is, like his poetry, filled with images, he is here speaking of something that I recognize in myself, something that applies in all human experience:

> Inside, in the dark of the stone, it feels as if you are sustaining a great pressure, bowing down like the generations of monks who must have bowed down in meditation and reparation on the floor ... But coming out of the cold heart of the stone into the sunlight and dazzle of grass and sea, I felt a lift in my heart, a surge towards happiness that must have been experienced by those monks as they crossed that same threshold centuries ago.[3]

Much of the poetry that these early hermits left gives a picture of the beauty and happiness of their lives, and these are of course the poems most commonly reproduced in anthologies and quoted by those writing on the Celtic celebration of creation. But they also wrote about the price that they paid in pain and darkness in their desert time just as Fr Christian did. It is because they do not deny what is harsh and cruel in nature that they can also write of its joyousness.

> Grey branches have wounded me,
> they have torn my hands.

Here the hermit experiences existential loneliness: 'all alone I came into the world, alone I shall go from it' and an eighth-century hermit rule speaks of what this will mean:

A cold anxious bed, like the lying-down of the doomed, a brief apprehensive sleep, cries frequent and early.[4]

ᖇᖇ᯽ᖅᖅ

It is good to be in touch with nature. But it is also tempting to idealize it. Those who actually live close to the earth, who work with the soil, are not sentimental about it. The reality is that nature is unpredictable, often cruel and merciless. It is good to enjoy the natural world, but it is important to see it not only with enjoyment but with clarity. For God only works with reality. When in the 1970s Philip Toynbee read something which said that the whole creation was dancing in eternal joy with God himself the principal dancer he wrote furiously in his journal:

> Alas, such rhapsodies are meaningless to me; worse than meaningless – self-indulgent falsification. For it is not *true* that the whole creation dances in eternal joy: ask the mouse as the owl's talons clutch it: ask the child dying alone after the earthquake . . . We do not want to see only the natural world that is prettified, shorn of pain and disfigurement, in which there is no room for blood or bone. If we fail to take the pain of creation seriously we also fail to take the reality of God seriously.[5]

As I allow my outer landscape to play its part in shaping my inner landscape I must take this lesson to heart. It is tempting to see the idyll of the gentle rolling hills and the fields of grazing flocks that surround my home in the Welsh Marches and forget that these same hills and fields were the battle-torn and fought-over lands and the scene for centuries of bitter conflict. Peter Levi, in his book *Flutes of Autumn*,[6] in which he writes so lyrically and poignantly of the English landscape, reminds us that there is hardly an acre of English countryside which is not blood-stained. The monuments in our churches and the war memorials standing on our village greens never allow us to forget those who died fighting for their country in foreign lands, on the Somme or in South Africa. But we do not so often choose to remember the blood of our own people, spilt on our own soil. Those times of violence, pain, suffering, the unhealed wounds of history, are smoothed out and prettified for the tourist and sightseer.

It is interesting to find that the author of those best-selling children's books, the Harry Potter series, says that although some of the things which happen in her stories may be upsetting they are not damaging. 'If you are going to examine evil actions then you have a moral obligation not to fudge the issue.' Perhaps one of the reasons for J. K. Rowling's widespread popularity may be the fact that she refuses to fudge issues of good and evil and that it is not only her young readers who recognize it and are grateful.

Things go wrong; we live with evil and weakness and failure and sin, a mutilated world. Many will remember that in the week following 11 September 2001 the *New Yorker* published a poem by the Polish poet Adam Zagajewski with the significant title 'Try to Praise the Mutilated World', in which he holds on to the abiding memories of what is there underlying disaster, telling us to recall moments of blessing. (I shall refer to it again in Chapter 8, 'Gift'.) Nothing is to be gained by denial. Yet it is wrong to stay with the black memories. Things that are painful must be brought out into the open and faced, faced in the right way so that they will lead us forward.

The Celtic world understood the sorrow that makes for joy. They knew too the value of tears, and prayed for the gift of tears, tears that were not morbid or guilt-ridden, but cleansing and refreshing, and above all freeing. Do we weep today for our sins? Do we even speak of sin? In *The Cocktail Party* T. S. Eliot puts these words into the mouth of Celia when we first meet her:

> Well, my upbringing was pretty conventional –
> I had always been taught to disbelieve in sin.
> Oh, I don't mean that it was never mentioned!
> But anything wrong, from our point of view,
> Was either bad form, or was psychological.[7]

Rather than weeping is it not much more likely that either we live in fear, attempting to bury what we cannot face, or that we become worried and anxious, trying to find something outside ourselves (family or upbringing, environment, 'the system') to blame and so shift the responsibility? In one of her broadcast talks Lavinia Byrne gave this warning: 'Spirituality and psychology have lain down together like the lion and the lamb. We have danced, prayed, sung and massaged our way to wholeness.' This however is an understandable reaction to that disastrous linking of sin and guilt, which was the message that many of the churches, both Protestant or Catholic, gave out and which did so much harmful damage to so many people, encouraging them to dwell on their sinfulness with an almost obsessive regret or guilt, endlessly reviewing past failings and becoming trapped in unhealthy introspection and self-analysis.

But, as so often, the monastic tradition brings us into a fuller picture. St Benedict couples sin and a saving God. He will not compromise on how serious a matter sin is; he tells us that we have 'departed' from God. But he takes this crack, which is deep and pervasive both at the heart of the world and of our own selves, and shows us that it can become a *felix culpa*, a happy fault. Confronting us with the compromised truth about ourselves he forces us to face it and to deal with it. If I look honestly into the depths of my own self I cannot fail to see sin, to be aware of my failings, and the way in which this happens time and again. It is humbling to stand before God with our failures, wounds, chaos, vulnerability. I think we all know deep down that it is only by facing them that we can hope to enlighten the darkness. This means that we must start by grieving honestly and without pretence or excuse.

'Sorrow is at least an arriving' Fr Vincent tells the sorrowful old man Kumalo in Alan Paton's famous novel set in apartheid South Africa, *Cry the Beloved Country*, 'Fear impoverishes always, while sorrow may enrich.' His son has killed a white man, a very good white man, and when he responds that he cannot feel that he is enriched, Father Vincent says again 'Sorrow is better than fear. Fear is a journey, a terrible journey, but sorrow is at least an arriving.'[8]

It is only when we can stand before God, weak and in need of mercy, without any pretence or facade, that then we can hope for acceptance and healing. The very first image which is given us in those opening words of the Rule, *Listen my son*, is that of the prodigal, St Benedict reminding us that we too have strayed, have wasted the good heritage given to us, and instead find ourselves eating empty husks. The significant moment in this story is when the prodigal faces that reality, and as the fog clouding his inner vision lifts he sees exactly where he is and what he is doing. So he begins the journey home. That return reveals so much about God as father, as he throws dignity to the winds, and rushes out to meet his son and cuts short those carefully prepared words of penitence. This is also the story of each of us, and it does not happen once, but time and again throughout our lives. The key lies in *metanoia*, that moment of grace when the truth about ourselves and God strikes us, piercing the heart and making a new life possible.

'The piercing of the heart' is a good description of compunction, which I find one of the most valuable and practical concepts which the monastic tradition brings us. The word itself comes from the Latin *punctio*, to penetrate, to puncture, to wound. We are wounded simultaneously by two things: by God's love for us and by our failure to respond to that love. Compunction is like a sharp dart, which is of course a dart of love, and which as it pierces the heart shows me with sudden awareness how I have been false to my own deepest and truest self. I am stricken at my compromised and feeble response to this outpouring of love. This awareness however, in the monastic tradition, carries nothing of morbid self-absorption and scrupulosity. Sorrow that is negative, anxious, regressive is backward looking, and will bear no fruit. I have thus to be at the same time strong and vulnerable, strong enough to see and to feel my real state without self-deception and to resolve that I will try to respond more fully to that generous love, yet vulnerable enough to let my tears wash away my protective defences and leave me open and willing for God to work on me.

❦

Tears, O my God, who but you will give me?

The early Fathers, both in the West and the East, like the Celtic monks, had much to say about tears, the gift of tears, the mystery of tears, but above all the right and wrong tears. They saw them as a gift for which it was proper to pray and which, like all gifts, must be used properly. In the Celtic tradition people would ask that a well of tears spring up in their hearts, or that a stream would reach every part, flowing and becoming a cleansing for heart and body. A tenth-century Irish poem has the constant repetition of the plea 'Grant me tears':

> Grant me tears when rising, grant me tears when resting, beyond your every gift altogether for love of you, Mary's Son.[9]

The theme of tears encourages striking images:

> By weeping a door is opened through which we enter.

> Wash your face, flood it with tears so that it may shine with glory before God. A face bathed with tears has an undying beauty.

> Anyone who has no inward sorrow and who is never moved to tears is like a child not yet born who remains in the womb, compared to an adult at full manly stature.

Tears falling as rain on the grass and showers on the herb causing knowledge to grow up for the harvest and the multiplying of its grains.

Tears have the taste of wine; tears are like fire and water, purifying. Echoing the words of Psalms 66: 'We went through fire and through water, yet you have brought us forth to a spacious place.'[10]

But St Athanasius gives this timely warning: 'There are many who wept over their sins but forgot the purpose of tears.' The purpose is to move from contrition, deeply felt, to the response to freeing and forgiving love.

❦

Standing in front of a bookstall at the back of a church in America I thought about this when I saw that the title of a book of essays by Rowan Williams originally called *Open to Judgement* had been changed to *A Ray of Darkness*.[11] I spent a moment or two turning that juxtaposition of words into a prayer for myself. I wanted to stay with that image, and to play with it, and to recall that I had read how Fr Christian had placed a crucifix in his Algerian chapel in which the nails which pierced the hands of Christ sent out rays. I wanted to stand at the foot of that cross and believe that the darkness of the cross is a promise of light and love, piercing the darkness with a love beyond all failure and betrayal.

Perhaps in the end we ought to speak of 'the mystery of tears'. These are grace-making tears. The path to happiness begins with these tears. Compunction brings blessing. St John Chrysostom tried to draw his hearers to compunction with these words:

Joy is not contrary to mourning; it is even born from it. He who weeps for his evil deeds and admits them is in joy. To put the same thing in another way: it is possible to be in mourning for one's own sins and in joy because of Christ.[12]

So the issue now becomes: how do I respond to this invitation to new life, an invitation springing from love? Newness can only come from a grief articulated and embraced. The least that I can do is to show in some practical way that it has truly touched me. The response comes in *metanoia* or repentance. It means that I see with clarity, I weep for what is wrong, in order that I may turn around, resolved to do better. For if the end and purpose of our life is the joy of the resurrection, being transformed into the likeness of Christ (the theme of transformation which came in the previous chapter) then I am being taken forward, into new energy, new life. I love the vigour with which Abbot Isaiah says:

> Sadness according to God does not weigh on the
> >   soul,
> but says to it, 'Do not be afraid! Up! Return!'
> God knows that man is weak,
> and strengthens him.[13]

I like to take the word *reorientation* and remind myself that it implies the turning towards the rising sun or towards the new light – which is the theme that I am exploring today. This was something that Philip Toynbee recognized with gratitude when he said that Christ does not merely lighten the burden of our sins (a phrase which he as so many others has never been able to cope with) but lightens them by shining his light on them.[14] God's gaze is the gaze of a loving father from whom no secrets are hidden, the gaze which lights up all the dark and hidden corners of my heart. It is a shaft of light penetrating all my defences, whose purpose is not to judge in the sense of any legal process but rather to enlighten what is wrong in order to heal and to restore. God wants us to recognize what is true because only the truth can set us free.

Rembrandt, in his painting of the prodigal, has caught the gaze on the father's face, and then as we turn to look at those two hands placed on the son's shoulders, we see the one so firm and strong, the other so gentle. There is a parallel here in those two eyes of Christ in a famous icon in St Catharine's Sinai: one looking with a penetrating clarity, the other with deep compassion. There is no escape from that loving gaze, even though I turn my back. In an extraordinary sermon, such as only he was capable of preaching, Austin Farrer speaks of those eyes and those hands, and how strong is a love which refuses to give up in spite of all resistance and every failure to respond:

> My back is turned to him,
> I have been told that he forgives me,
> but I will not turn
> and have the forgiveness,
> even though I feel the eyes on my back.
> But God does not give up:
> for he takes my head between his hands
> and turns my face to make me smile at him.
>
> . . .
>
> He has taken a pair of human hands
> with which to turn our stiff-necked heads,
> and bring our eyebeams
> into line with his own.[15]

The art of the icon catches God's gaze in a way that no other expression, either by word or image, could possibly do. I realized this particularly vividly as I stood before Rublev's icon of the Trinity in the Tretakov gallery in Moscow in the company of a Russian priest. He could put it into the context of the turbulent history of his country, and could tell me how it came out of the suffering of his people. And Rowan Williams in his poem 'Rublev' gives us these words, as though Rublev himself is speaking:

> I said, Here is the blood of all our people,
> these are their bruises, blue and purple,
> gold, brown, and pale green wash of death.[16]

As a result I became aware of the significance of something that I had hitherto scarcely registered, the small square, at the level of my eye. This table is an altar, and in the front is the place where the relics of the martyrs were put – those who had responded so totally to the question which the scene above asks 'Can you drink of this cup?' So the icon carries the question that comes to any of us: 'Can you drink of this cup?'

The three figures of the Trinity all point towards that central cup; the suffering of the martyrs pointed them towards Christ. They are telling us that there is a right and a wrong way of suffering. My response to the question of the icon must never be one that will draw me inwards, but instead draw me into the participation in that loving and intimate gaze of love which the Trinitarian Godhead shows us.

Darkness and suffering are inevitable, inescapable, often appearing unexpectedly, without warning, at any point in our lives, coming as someone said 'like an emotional thunderbolt'. Loss or bereavement, accidents and disasters, physical and psychological pain can take every sort of form and context: illnesses like Alzheimer's or cancer, the ending of a relationship, bankruptcy, loss, war, famine, exile – each of us can make our own list. But what frequently compounds the suffering, and makes it even more damaging, is the way it frequently seems to be so unjust. Then it is tempting to feed on hurt and anger, and today's litigious society, which seeks financial compensation for every kind of supposed injury, can easily encourage the determination to squeeze out as much as possible from it. It might actually become a rather satisfying meal – until at some point it becomes apparent that I am feeding on myself and I have become the skeleton at the feast.[17]

How then are we to approach suffering? How are we to prevent suffering from being negative and destructive? Is it possible to make it positive? Can we learn from, even gain from suffering? For surely the most terrible thing about it is its utter pointlessness. In his autobiography Harry Williams tells very honestly of the time at Cambridge when he suffered a nervous breakdown:

> The more of a dead-end it feels the more is it an invitation to join in Christ's sufferings ... So the cruelly destructive and negative nature of suffering can be seen, if only in a glass very darkly, as charged with positive and creative possibilities.[18]

When one is at the lowest point of apparently meaningless darkness, when life seems to be negative and without direction, all those comforting assurances that 'all will be well' seem only to trivialize and patronize. There is one thing alone to hold on to, and that is that our God is himself a suffering God and that he is there in the place of suffering with us. Since everyone's experience of suffering is totally unique, it becomes inappropriate to speak too much about it, yet this is how a close friend who had cancer wrote about it in a letter to me:

> I have learnt a lot in my body about Christ's passion. You will not think this blasphemous of me I trust. I have decided that the essence of his passion was in his 'passiveness', his being done to, as it were ... I thought of the Lord's silence in the face of bodily humiliations. He gave his back to the smiters as Isaiah puts it. My spiritual task in the midst of the physical illness was to give my self to it, to relinquish control,

to be passive in the face of invasive and embarrassing procedures. It has been a strange grace.

As this chapter begins to reach its end I am still faced by the mystery of pain, and even more by the mystery of the transforming power of pain. At the Lambeth Conference of 1998, on the feast of the Transfiguration, Susan Cole-King, whose father had suffered most cruelly at the hands of the Japanese during the war, spoke of what she had learnt from that experience of the transfiguring power of suffering. She ended by quoting Karl Barth:

> Thus our tribulation, without ceasing to be tribulation, is transformed. We suffer as we suffered before, but our suffering is no longer a passive perplexity but is transformed into a pain which is creative, fruitful, full of power and promise. The road which was impassable has been made known to us in the crucified and risen Lord.[19]

The psalms allow us to lament, to cry out in pain and anguish. But they also effect a transformation. As we pray or sing, or shout them, the psalms use the strong language which does not try to pretend that we are nice. So we can groan, complain bitterly, tell God how unfair his actions are, indulge in bitter grief and reveal all our mental hurts and despair. All the sadnesses that wash over us, and all the feelings of anger and resentment, all those violent feelings, and not least when they become ugly and bitter, are here expressed without any apology or pretence. Even the saying of these hateful things out loud is a way of acknowledging them, and of turning them over to God. If we know that we are being listened to by this God then we are at least standing in a place where God's healing can also begin.

Thomas Merton in his book on the psalms, *Bread in the Wilderness*, says that at the very moment of distress and anguish as we enter into the action of the psalms

> we allow ourselves to be absorbed in the spiritual agony of the Psalmist and of the One he represented, and allowed their sorrows to be swallowed up in the sorrows of this mysterious Personage and then they found themselves swept away on the strong tide of his hope, into the very depths of God.

So a transformation is effected, a transformation which is more than a mere catharsis, as fear is turned into fortitude, and anguish somehow becomes joy without ceasing to be anguish, and we triumph over suffering not by escaping it but by completely accepting it.

'There is no victory in evasion.' Merton sums up in those few simple words what I have been trying to explore in this chapter. It is not an answer to pain and suffering. There is no answer. But we walk alongside Christ and believe and hope that we too shall come through this as he himself did:

> We lift up our heads in the valley of the shadow
> and we draw breath,
> and light momentarily trembles in our eyes
> that have been too long filled with the waters of
> death.
> Then our spirit cracks the walls of its tomb with
> something of the power
> Christ shed into our souls
> on the morning of his resurrection.[20]

Amongst all that has been said on this subject one voice stands out for me. I like to think of Helen Luke in the genre of old wise woman. In the final chapter of her book, *Old Age, Journey into*

Simplicity, as she writes about suffering, and she has shown me how to turn from the unproductive and neurotic to the positive and liberating by speaking of how we should *embrace* suffering. By this she means that we should carry it, rather than lying down under its weight and letting ourselves be crushed by it. She showed me how all the terms, affliction, grief, depression bring images of weight bearing down: to be afflicted is to be struck down by a blow; grief is derived from *gravare*, and to be depressed is to be pressed down. But she tells us that if we can possibly pass through this door into 'the fiercer suffering' a strange thing may happen:

> We have lifted the weight and instead of being crushed by it, we find it is extraordinarily light – 'My yoke is easy, my burden is light.' The pain remains but it is more like the piercing of a sword than a weight.[21]

I find a parallel between her words and the picture that Stanley Spencer painted of Christ carrying the cross through the main street of his native village, Cookham in Berkshire. We are told that he gave it the title *carrying* rather than bearing quite deliberately because 'he particularly wished to convey the relationship between the carpenters behind him carrying the ladders and Christ in front carrying the cross, each doing their job of work'. Spencer believed that by entering into our humanity Christ gave human life great dignity, and made all human tasks and human experience worthy, even holy. For this reason he placed the scene in the midst of busy, cheerful village life. 'Quite suddenly I became aware that everything was full of special meaning and this made everything holy.'[22]

'He showed them his hands and his side. Then the disciples rejoiced when they saw the Lord' (John 20.20). A week later Christ will say to Thomas: '*Put* your finger here and see my hands.

Reach out your hand and put it into my side.' Christ is offering his wounds not only to be seen but to be entered into. These words were addressed to Thomas, doubter, the uncertain one, but they also speak to any of us. Yet *noli me tangere* is also true too. The risen Christ says to Mary 'Do not hold on to me, stop clinging to me.' He does not say 'Do not touch', for touching is important – even if it is no more than touching the hem of the robe. Clinging, however, suggests the wrong sort of dependency, a holding on to what is passing, instead of looking forward – or, as we see portrayed in the statue of Mary by Elisabeth Frink which stands outside Salisbury Cathedral, to striding vigorously forward into the future.

After he had spent the night wrestling, Jacob ended up with a new name, a name which carried a new vision, a new vocation. Here is the promise that I too can hope to win through to new life. It strikes me afresh when I read the story as re-told by Keith Ward:

> Jacob walked slowly across the river, his mind numb and confused. 'Last night' he thought 'I fought with a man until the breaking of the day. But what was it I fought? My own fear? A demon of the river? Or was it the one who knows me through and through, who has given me a new name and his blessing, who calls me to pursue his promise and follow his way?'[23]

Jacob leaves limping, but he does at least move forward, unlike Lot's wife who is turned into a pillar of salt because she cannot stop gazing at what she has lost. Sometimes we may be faced with a dramatic night-long struggle with darkness, sometimes we simply face the quieter struggle of daily trials and difficulties, which Helen Luke calls 'the day-to-day onslaughts of hurt feelings, black moods, exhaustion'.[24] This is the choice: to walk forward courageously or to look back and cling to what is no longer there. Do we need a poet to tell us that we can never return to the past? Of course there is a deep longing to return to Eden. But Edwin Muir, born into the paradise of an Orkney island where men and women and children were at one, and then forced because of poverty to leave, reminds us in his poem 'One Foot in Eden' that Eden has to go. But in its place come 'strange blessings' as blackened trees give way to new blossoms, not innocence restored but something new and different:

> But famished field and blackened tree
> Bear flowers in Eden never known.
> Blossoms of grief and charity
> Bloom in those darkened fields alone.[25]

So this day ends not with any easy answers but with the confidence of the poet who tells us that from the darkened fields will come new flowers, blossoms that we could never have imagined.

Prayers and Reflections

Blessed are those whose strength is in you,
in whose heart are your ways,
who trudging through the plains of misery
find in them an unexpected spring,
a well from deep below the barren ground,
and the pools are filled with water.

They become springs of healing for others,
reservoirs of compassion to those who are bruised.
Strengthened themselves they lend courage to
                                        others,
and God will be there at the end of their journey.

Psalm 84

Come, then, Lord my God,
come and instruct my heart
where and how to search·for you,
where and how to find you.
Where shall I look for you, Lord?

                    . . .

O Lord, you are my Lord and my God, and I have never
seen you.
You have made and remade me
and bestowed on me all the good that I possess . . .
Give thyself to me again
so that all may be well with me
for without you everything goes wrong for me.

Look kindly upon my labours,
my striving do come to you,
for apart from you. I can do nothing.

St Anselm, *Proslogion*

I find myself in the primordial
lostness of night, solitude,
forest, peace, a mind
awake in the dark ... In the
formlessness of night and silence
a word then
pronounces itself: Mercy.

Thomas Merton

The Myrrhbearers came
(with what fear and trembling?)
trudging along in darkness
worrying about
the stone.

Everybody worries about
the stone,
the great impediment
between us
and what we seek,

that great burden
we carry
like Sisyphus
laboring
up and down the hill.

The sun rose.
The women looked up.
The stone,
which was very large,
had been removed.

No wonder they ran
to tell Cephas.
Somebody should tell Sisyphus:
'Put it down, man,
and dance on it.'

Bonnie Thurston

My soul pines for you,
My soul clings to you, and your right hand bears me
up.

However, this very exhaustion and pining away
have a strengthening effect upon the soul.
A thirsty person wants to spend all his time beside a
fountain.
It seems as if his one desire is to be thoroughly
drenched by it
so that by this means his thirst may be assuaged.
And so Lord, your right hand bears me up and
strengthens me,
making a new person of me, and enabling me to say:
It is no longer I who live,
but Christ who lives in me.

St Ambrose

The road pointed out to you is not a long one;
you do not have to cross the seas
or pierce the clouds
or climb mountains to meet your God.
Enter into you own soul and you will find him,
for *his word is near you*;
it is on your lips and in your heart.
Go down deep into your heart
until you are stirred to compunction.

St Bernard, *Sermon*

Compunction . . .
transforms those who receive it.
A bubbling fountain springs up in their midst,
which is the water of life,
ever leaping and welling up
and watering them abundantly.

St Symeon the New Theologian

O God, my God, look upon me,
why have you forsaken me?
When this God-Word had become flesh,
he hung upon the cross and cried,
My God, my God, look upon me,
why have you forsaken me?
For what other reason was this said than that
WE WERE THERE?
Nos ibi eramus. Why did he say it,
unless he was somehow trying to catch our attention,
to make us understand that
'This psalm is written about me'?

St Augustine, preaching in Holy Week on Psalm 21

On hills, in valleys, on the islands of the sea,
Wherever you may go
Because of the holy cross there is no desert place.

Black Book of Carmarthen

We shall through patience share in the sufferings of Christ –
that we may deserve also to share in his kingdom. Amen.

Prologue, *The Rule of St Benedict*

7

Mystery

'I am content to stay with mystery.' This was the response of the guide taking tourists round the great prehistoric chamber tomb of Knowth in the Boyne valley in Ireland when they asked him about its purpose, and the meanings of the dynamic abstract designs which decorate its huge rock slabs. Of course we will go on asking questions, but I hope that I will also be content to stay with that answer, and I shall be happy to accept that in the end the thought patterns of these ancient Celtic people and the way in which they saw their universe will continue to elude me, in spite of all the advances of academic scholarship. When Mary Oliver, the American poet, says that she feels that we have been not just educated, but possibly over-educated, I feel the same. 'Knowledge has entertained me, shaped me and it has failed me' she says, there is still more to discover which the world of learning will never bring us. 'Something in me still starves.'[1]

It is a natural impulse to wish to complete something, to round it off satisfactorily, to bring it to an end. Yet there is also a place for the imperfect, the unfinished, and this serious point is made in light-hearted fashion by a Benedictine monk, Fr Kilian McDonnell when he writes about 'Perfection':

> I have had it with perfection
> I have packed my bags
> I am out of here
> Gone.

. . .

Perfection straineth out
the quality of mercy,
withers rapture at its
birth.

Hints I could have taken –
even the perfect chiselled form of
Michelangelo's David
squints.

The Venus de Milo
has no arms
the Liberty Bell is cracked.[2]

What is fragmentary, glimpsed or half-glimpsed, can have an important role to play in this retreat as in my daily life. Poets who give us 'snatches of music rather than complete songs' bring us something important.[3] So if at the end of this time I still find that I am asking questions I should see that as a sign of maturity and be happy to accept I am not always going to have answers. The peculiar nature of questions, as Philip Toynbee said, is that they do not have the same limiting character as answers and statements:

if one can ask a question and not expect an answer,
if one can look at a mystery and not expect it to be
revealed,
if one can look at the veil of consciousness and not
expect it to be lifted.[4]

Pause – take time – do not fill up all the spaces.

Everything in this retreat so far has brought me to this point: silence, listening, gazing, taking time, attentiveness, wonder. Those huge Irish prehistoric tombs have given me the natural starting point for today's theme of mystery, for the Celtic world is at once familiar but also ultimately unknown. In recent years I am so grateful that I have come to discover the Celtic tradition, above all in Wales and Ireland where I have not only travelled widely but also tried to read widely. Yet I feel in the end I have encountered a people whose imagination eludes me and will continue to elude me. As Celtic interest widens and increasing numbers of people become enthusiasts for all things Celtic, I think we should recall the words of a man who was arguably the most distinguished Welsh poet of our day, R. S. Thomas:

> You can come in
> You can come a long way . . .
> But you won't be inside.

So I try to walk in reverence, taking off my shoes, remembering that this is holy ground, and having to accept that there is much that I shall never fully know and that may in the end be the most important gift of the Celts. I am left with questions about how they saw their world, how they interpreted the relationship of human and divine, the natural and the supernatural. When they built those great Irish monuments they were undoubtedly influenced by the movement of the sun and the moon, and by the alignment of the stars. Their abstract designs are at once primitive and sophisticated – and they continue to hold their secrets.

Celtic Christianity through its monasteries, the new patrons of the arts, took up the riches of this pre-Christian world and used it with verve and invention. The result is a subtle and sophisticated art which expressed the Christian faith visually and with huge vitality. This extraordinary artistic imagination was brought to bear on whatever material they were handling, whether a gigantic rock slab or the delicate filigree work of a chalice or a bell cover. Delighting in the fluidity of pattern they loved to use convolutions and spirals, knots and flowing curves. It was commonly said that the Celtic soul was adverse to anything square or straight.

Irish Celtic Christianity excelled in expressing the faith in symbols, metaphors, images, both visual and poetic. Their powers of imagination were astonishing. They have given us a rich complexity in which it is tempting to search for meaning, or perhaps double meaning, even though it may actually be that no meaning at all was intended. Of course the scholars must continue with their researches in an attempt to interpret, to ascertain the context and connections. But perhaps we should ask ourselves if much of this was not simply playful – and maybe take that to heart ourselves. On the high cross at Monasterboice in Ireland we find two cats sitting at the base of the cross, and two men tugging at one another's beards on the side, and I refuse to find anything significant here other than that the men who built this were enjoying themselves.

The high crosses of Ireland remain unique among the artistic achievements of Christendom. They are ringed crosses rising from a huge plinth which ends in a cap stone. The great circular O is held in the centre of the cross by the outstretched arms on either side. Only when we approach them with an open mind that is close to awe, not simply for the structural achievement, though this is impressive, but for the symbolic statements that they make, can we begin to appreciate their significance. Here the circle, the globe of the world, is held is tension with the cross of the crucifixion – creation and redemption are brought together.

The massive foundation on which the whole structure of the cross depends is made up of two or three stepped slabs of rock, to recall Golgotha, the spot where traditionally the skull of Adam was buried and Christ was crucified. The cap stone at the head of the cross is modelled on the church of the resurrection in Jerusalem, and the main shaft of the cross which links them is the tree of life, so that we are brought from the depths and darkness of death and sin to the promise of new life. For the old adage was that as the human race fell by a tree so also were we rescued by a tree:

Thus the unholy wood (tree) the cause of sin becomes the cause of salvation, and the holy of holies, the place of skulls becomes the place where life is made.

It is not only that everything carried symbolic meaning, but layers of meaning. The ring which is a glory or halo around the head of Christ, carries further images: it may represent the rising sun, the laurel wreath of the victor, the circle of the cosmos, the whole created universe. Skilled in the handling of words as well as the handling of stone they exclaim:

> Behold the orb
> that shines with the rays of the sun,
> which the cross of salvation spreads from its
> height,
> embracing the earth, the sea,
> the winds and the sky.[5]

The entire cross depends on the figure of Christ placed at the centre of the circle which comes at the centre of the cross. This suffering Christ is also Christus Victor, the hero warrior, a figure who would mean so much to a tribal people, the one who fights to defend and free his people, who will take on and defeat the forces of evil and darkness that were so real to them. He holds out his arms, with huge, over-sized hands, the Hand of God, to bless and rescue the world that he has both created and redeemed. And then sometimes Christ will be clothed in the long white robe of the risen Christ so that the crucified and the risen Christ are one.

Of course, the crosses played an important part in the liturgical life of the monastic community when they would gather here as part of their regular life of prayer and praise. The singing of the Benedicite, for example, the song of the three young men in the fiery furnace, praising God in the midst of suffering, would have been very immediate to the men and women standing in front of the panel which depicted this poplar scene, showing the young men, the flames and above their head the angel.

Unless one is willing to spend time with a Celtic high cross it will be impossible for it to *unveil* its many layers of meaning – a word that I used at the start of this book and which I return to again and again. These ambiguities and half-glimpsed perceptions are not unlike the word-juggling of James Joyce or like the poetic language which has always been close to the Celtic temperament. Irish writers were fond of the expression 'to see with the eyes of the heart', a good metaphor for what was undoubtedly intended by these early monastic builders and patrons. Onlookers with different educations and interests would find different meanings there, just as we can return to these crosses time after time and see things that are new. These are living stones; a Celtic high cross captures truth which resists closure.

Here again we are facing mystery for, above all, the cross stands both for the person and the symbol of Christ in an interchangeable way. Christ is not only raised up on the cross but also raised up in the resurrection and the ascension, which have become one single thing. It is that single event which is the Glory of which that great central circle speaks. It is not of course the cross itself which is glorious but Christ himself who is glorious.

'The pattern of the glory' is one of the most characteristic phrases of Charles Williams, whose writings themselves belong to no single category. He used fiction, poetry, history, literary criticism, essays, because, as T. S. Eliot understood, he had to say what was beyond his resources, and probably beyond the resources of language. Glory for him was amazement, brightness, like seeing through a kaleidoscope. But it is not a hazy blur, that indistinctiveness which turns mystery into mystification. Like a solemn liturgy or an intricate dance, there is an all-inclusive orderliness, a network, as each thing is connected to the other in a vastly complex web of interdependence. That is why he speaks of the *pattern* of the glory and not just the glory. And why he insists that the 'glory of God is in the facts'.

> The almost incredible nature of things is that there is no fact which is not in his glory.

An American critic who has made a study of Charles Williams's work has helped to elucidate this for me when he says that the best analogy is in the understanding of poetry:

> God is the poet, and the world, past and present, is the poem. If this universal poem is to be rightly construed, all the words – every fact – must be accounted for. Each has a place in the whole and none may be overlooked. And if it is to be construed in terms of its author's intention, as a poem should be, the terms must be God's rather than ours, 'the terms he deigns to apply, not the terms we force on him.'[6]

ᏫᎬᎤᎯᎯ

The great thirteenth-century cosmati pavement which lies in front of the high altar of Westminster Abbey is a galaxy of shapes and colours, inscriptions and patterns created from materials drawn from all corners of the then known world. Lying on a bed of Purbeck marble it contains purple porphyry, the only known source of which is the eastern desert of Egypt; green serpentine coming from quarries near Sparta on the Greek mainland; a yellow limestone known as *giallo antico* quarried in north west Africa. Its basic layout is a fourfold symmetry, but then within that there is an endless and dazzling variety. The four roundels are circular, octagonal, hexagonal, heptagonal; the bands which link them differ in pattern and colour; while a complex geometry plays inexhaustibly with numbers. The third inscription running round the middle circle reads: SPERICUS: ARCHETIPIM: GLOBUS: HIC: MONSTRAT: MACROCOSMUM; *The Spheri-*

cal globe here shows the archetypal macrocosm. This is therefore the great world in which we live, the microcosm being humankind.

Just as there can simultaneously be layer upon layer of significance in the tombs or the high crosses, so also we find here several levels can be present. It was this ability to shift and shimmer through layers of meaning that gave medieval symbolism its rich vitality. Designs were a potential for multiple resources, for a labyrinth of significance. Nor does our present-day interpretation necessarily tell us what it meant to its original creators. The question of the men who made it was not 'How does the world work?' but 'What does it mean?' It plays with numbers, for example, all of which carry symbolic meaning; it includes the colours of the four elements, fire, air, water and earth; it points to the four points of the compass. But even the sophistication of contemporary scholarship cannot reveal all its secrets, and in the end they must still remain mysterious.[7]

'Wonder upon wonder' – Giraldus Cambrensis the twelfth-century Welsh traveller stood in amazement at his first sight of the *Book of Kells*, the Irish book of the Gospels made sometime around the year 900, and described in the annals of Ulster in 1000 as the 'chief treasure of the western world'. He felt himself caught up in the beauty and intricacy of its design. The longer he gazed at it, the more he was drawn into its depths and what lay hidden there. In 1989, centuries later, when the carpet that had covered the great marble pavement at Westminster Abbey was rolled back for the first time in more than a century the reaction of those who saw it was the same. For the three days that it was left uncovered more than 7,000 people filed around the edge of the pavement. It was as though they were held spellbound, complaining when they had to be ushered on because of the queue stretching back into the forecourt of the abbey itself that they needed more time for their eyes and minds to drink in its fascination. The historian of the pavement Richard Foster who observed this, later wrote in his study of the pavement about what pattern-making can do and how it allows the mind to move, by analogy and extrapolation, 'beyond the understanding of things directly perceived to conceptions of matters as yet unknown'.[8]

The medieval mind delighted in endlessly playing with shapes and numbers, incorporating them into ever more new and intricate designs. They followed the early fifth-century B C Greek thinking and presented the four elements in two pairs of opposing qualities: fire is dry and hot; air is hot and moist; water is moist and cold; earth is cold and dry, so that each shares a quality with two of the others, and in this way what might seem to be opposites become united in a stable and well-tuned harmony. Illuminated manuscripts would be adorned with decorative foliate interlacing which was a visual expression of harmony. Windows, wall paintings and pavements of the great European cathedrals offered space and scope for playing with ideas. It is difficult today to begin to regain a sense of the power contained in this symbolic dimension of the world, though we probably glimpse it most easily in the context of a medieval cathedral. The nave, seen as the gateway to heaven spoke of earthly life, and was therefore the appropriate setting for the labyrinth which represents humanity's earthly journey towards salvation while the chancel and sanctuary spoke of heaven. The description that we have of the dedication of the new choir of Canterbury cathedral in 1130, in the presence of the king and the nobles of the realm, seemed to the contemporary mind more splendid than anything since the dedication of the temple of Solomon. The assembly chanted the liturgical 'Awesome is this place. Truly, this is the house of God and the gate of Heaven, and it will be called the court of the Lord'.

For this was a world where beauty mattered. The purpose of art and architecture was to reveal the beauty of God and of the divine order.

> God brings about an order
> that is always good order,
> and that consists in a beauty
> that imitates his own nature.[9]

Good order and beauty ask of the onlooker an attitude of reverence and respect and a certain humility, a willingness to take time, and to standing back – perhaps even to take off our shoes and go barefoot. This was something that Thomas Merton understood, as we see from his description of his visit to the huge Buddhist figures at Polannaruwa in Ceylon. The vicar-general who was accompanying him shied away from 'paganism', preferring to stay behind and read the guide book under a tree. So he approached alone, barefoot and undisturbed, and found that he was almost knocked over with a rush of thankfulness at the variety and fluidity of shape and line, and above all the silence of those extraordinary faces with their huge, subtle smiles, 'filled with every possibility, questioning nothing, knowing everything'. He was suddenly and forcibly jerked out of 'the habitual, half-tied vision of things':

> I know and have seen what I was obscurely looking for. I don't know what else remains but I have now seen and have pierced through the surface and have gone beyond the shadow and the disguise . . . It says everything, it needs nothing. And because it needs nothing it can afford to be silent, unnoticed, undiscovered.[10]

⁗⁗

Is it safer to read *about* something than to be challenged by the reality of the thing itself? The guidebook which Merton rejected and left in the hands of a member of the clerical hierarchy would have given him all the information. But it would have denied those figures their elusive and mysterious presence. Later Merton was to feel angry with himself for writing about it too quickly and for talking at a dinner party. Try to seize what any of these things 'mean' and they slip, they disappear – something that Frances Hororwitz knows when in the last two lines of her poem 'Winter Wood' she says:

We have encroached –
This is not yet our land.

Thomas Merton walked barefoot; Moses was told to take off
his shoes. How else can one approach mystery and respect it?
Moses in that marvellous and mysterious encounter with God
is told to stand barefoot. The image of taking off the shoes becomes the more significant when we remember that Moses would
in fact be being asked to undo the thongs of hide sandals, the
skins of dead animals, the deadness which prevents sensing the
reality of the earth under his feet. This is an image popular with
Jewish commentators who tell us that Moses was asked to divest
himself of two sandals, to untie all knots before coming to God.
They also remind us that he showed humility and hesitancy
when he replied that he was slow of speech and slow of tongue,
and only then was he ready to receive what the burning bush
brings.

꒰꜀꜡꜆꒱

The Desert Fathers delighted in the image of fire and flame:

Abba Joseph said to Abba Lot 'You cannot be a monk unless
you become a consuming fire'.

Abba Lot came to see Abba Joseph and said 'Father, according as I am able, I keep my little rule, and my little fast, my
prayer, meditation and contemplative silence; and according
as I am able I strive to cleanse my heart of thoughts; now
what more should I do?' The elder rose up in reply and
stretched out his hands to heaven, and his fingers became
like ten lamps of fire. He said: 'Why not be totally changed
into fire?'[11]

꒰꜀꜡꜆꒱

It is the poets above all who find delight in bringing together the bush, the fire, the flame. In *Aurora Leigh*, Elizabeth Barrett Browning tells us how she saw:

> Every burning bush a fire of God
> Like fire that alters everything
> On which it passes.

This transfiguring fire and flame show us God's creative and redeeming love over all his work, and we watch it taking place before our eyes. Here the Welsh poet James Nicholas sings to the bush:

> I sing to the bush, the flame of her beauty
> Catches the wind and sets fire to my song;
> It nourishes strength, it burns day and night,
> A triumphant fire:
>
> . . .
>
> I see her now lighting up my world.[12]

Or this poem by R. S. Thomas, 'The Bush':

> I know that bush,
> Moses; there are many of them
> in Wales in the autumn, braziers,
> where the imagination
> warms itself. I have put off
> pride and, knowing the ground
> holy, lingered to wonder
> how it is that I do not burn
> and yet am consumed.[13]

If we are to learn from the poets then we too must see that the ground is holy, take time to wonder, allow our imagination to warm itself. Perhaps this is as good a description of amazement and wonder – of astonishment! Thomas Traherne brought an 'astonished eye' to bear on the world around him, and for him

the bush and the fire become the instrument of transfiguration,
not just of the person but of the world itself:

> In every bush he sees a fire
>   In every Rock a spring,
> To quench the Thirst of his Desire,
>   His God in evrything.
> All Heaven descends, environs, enters him,
> He is Transfigured to a Seraphim.
>
> Being transformed, himself he is
>   A very Spring of Bliss.
> And everything he sees, his Ey
>   Doth Bless & Magnifie.
> His touch whatever it doth feel,
>   Be it or Stone or Steel,
> or Wood, or Earth, it turns it all to Gold;
> His Fingers pierce whatever thing they hold
>   In which it passes, he
> Doth to his own Blest Nature bring
>   The objects he doth see;
> They also burn, & turn to fire.[14]

In another poem Traherne takes the image of fire and flame
and applies it to the cross – and so to love:

> Tree set on
> fire with invisible flame,
> that Illuminateth all the World.   The Flame is
>   lov.[15]

This is the sort of illuminating connection that we find in Philip
Toynbee's journal as he discovered how seeing and loving
belonged together. He was of course a writer, a man who needed

words for the energy they brought him, but he also understood the limitations of words, or as he put it, the *burden* of words:

> Walking today, and tree-gazing I thought with real horror of trying to *write* about one of those well-studied trees ... any attempt to describe it would at once prejudice, betray the tree's superb and individual reality.[16]

How then are we to handle 'the mysteries which bewilder us so much'? How must we deal with 'the preposterous task of conceiving the inconceivable'? He played with images, knowing of course how easily they break down if one tries to elaborate them too much. He tries, for example, to write of that ever-present mystery of what he calls the 'eternal depth of the present moment':

> I imagined a great wooden ring slowly revolving,
> illuminated by a still lantern
> high up above its centre.
> We are all walking on the ring,
> as the ring itself is moving through time,
> our heads are usually bent down
> to watch the changing patterns of the grain.
> But sometimes we are able to catch a glimpse
> of the great central light,
> out of the corner of an eye.[17]

Writing just after his sixty-fourth birthday and looking forward to whatever was left of his life, he said that he hoped he might become increasingly aware of

> the presence of those holy mysteries which
> surround us all ...
> mysteries [that] are not problems to be solved
> but realities to be contemplated.[18]

꧁✿꧂

> Unless the eye catch fire
> The God will not be seen.

William Blake's familiar words sum it up. Am I looking inwards or outwards? Am I looking or *seeing*? A priest with a parish in London watches people walking along the pavements looking, searching for something, and says that it is as though the shop windows are mirrors showing them the reflection of themselves, so that what is happening is the bolstering of the ego-self. They were probably totally unaware of it, but they were looking inwards rather than turning outwards.[19]

Everything depends on whether, like Moses, we hear the voice of God asking us to take off our shoes and stand barefoot. This also means the stripping off of anything that might cloud our eyes and prevent us from seeing the world around as a cosmic burning bush. For Traherne this was essentially the gift that is there in childhood and is lost all too quickly later on. He tells us how

> all appeared New, and Strange at the first,
> inexpressibly rare,
> and Delightfull,
> and Beautifull.

All things were glorious, joyful and precious – then he asks:

> Is it not Strange that an Infant should be Heir of the World, and see those Mysteries which the Books of the Learned never unfold?

But he does of course want to find words to express the immensities of God and of the God-given world, and he writes in words that spill out, overflow, repeat, circle and dance. He, as it were, wastes time with words, piling them up on in cascading excitement. How else can he share with us his sense of the treasury which surrounds us, and in which we should be delighting?

It surroundeth us continually on every side,
it filles us,
and inspires us.
It is so Mysterious,
that it is wholly within us,
and even then it wholly seems,
and is without us.[20]

Things, like people, are never the same. 'Why do you watch the sunset daily?' the young man asked a monk on Patmos. And the monk replied, 'I am gathering fuel, I am collecting material, so that tonight as I pray I shall discover the presence of God in my own heart.'[21]

ᕯᕯᕯ

I have been trying to make this book a tapestry in which threads and themes weave in and out of one another, disappearing and then reappearing in a different context or another pattern. I also like to think of it as collage (a word that I found Mark Oakley had used although I did not know this at the time that I was writing), since a collage brings together shapes and colours and patterns, jostling and overlapping.[22] Threads, shadows, patchwork, glimpses – these shapes move and change. The biblical images are after all those which flicker: wind, flame, water, air. For this day, much of what I have been touching on is about exploring the reality that lies within and behind the visible world, about regaining our capacity to understand what is beyond words and beyond explanations. That is why abstract art has an important role to play. In a recent exhibition of his paintings Canon Robert Wright of Westminster Abbey quoted in its catalogue these words from Ouspensky:

There is no aspect of life that does not reveal to us an infinity of the new and unexpected if we approach it with the *knowledge* that is not exhausted by its visible aspect, that behind

Lost in Wonder

the visible there lies a whole world of the invisible, a world of forces and relations beyond our present comprehension.[23]

☙❦❧

All that I have been attempting to explore, in words that will always be inadequate, is here summed up very simply by Ben Okri:

> I think we need more
> of the wordless
> in our lives.
> We need more stillness,
> more of a sense of wonder,
> a feeling for the mystery of life.[24]

Prayers and Reflections

The God who draws me is urging me on,
and I discover my faltering Yes.
I stumble along the rough pathways,
surprised by a hand grasping my own.

To and fro, back and forth.
on the twists of the journey,

. . .

The hills themselves slowly change,
never as firm as they seem,
shrouded, brooding, and dark,
their rocks splintered by frost,
worn away by the lashing of storms.

Psalm 121

As you become more deeply attuned to the mystery of reality
. . . it teaches you things you can hardly put into words,
that can only be hinted by words to abandon the self
satisfaction of comfortable categories, to accept the unity
of opposites or contradictoriness) as the natural thing it
is in reality.

John Howard Griffin

A Stranger here
Strange Things doth meet, Strange Glories See;
Strange Treasures lodg'd in this fair World appear,
Strange all, and New to me.
But that they mine should be, who nothing was,
That Strangest is of all, yet brought to pass.

Thomas Traherne

Let not my humble presence affront and stumble
your hardened hearts that have not known my ways
nor seen my tracks converge to this uniqueness.
Mine is the strength of the hills that endure and crumble,
bleeding slow fertile dust to the valley floor.
I am the fire in the leaf that crisps and falls
and rots into the roots of the rioting trees.
I am the mystery, rising, surfacing
out of the seas into these infant eyes
that offer openness only and the unfocusing
search for an answering gaze. O recognize,
I am the undefeated heart of weakness.
Kneel to adore, fall down to pour your praise:
you cannot lie so low as I have been always.

John V. Taylor

God preserve us
from vision too explicit,
from compulsion to tell more
than can be understood.

Ruth Bidgood

What has the Lord in his goodness not done for us? He has made the whole of this perceptible universe a kind of mirror of heaven, so that by spiritual contemplation of the world around us we may reach up to heavenly things as if by some wonderful ladder.

St Gregory Palamas, *Homily*

Prayer is like watching for the
Kingfisher. All you can do is
Be there where he is likely to appear, and
Wait.
Often, nothing much happens;
There is space, silence and
Expectancy.
No visible sign, only the
Knowledge that he's been there,
And may come again.
Seeing or not seeing cease to matter,
You have been prepared.
But sometimes, when you've almost
Stopped expecting it,
A flash of brightness
Gives encouragement.

Ann Lewin, *Candles & Kingfishers*

The contemplative life has nothing to tell you
except to reassure you
and say that if you dare to penetrate your own
silence
and dare to advance without fear
into the solitude of your own heart . . .
you will truly recover the light and capacity
to understand what is beyond words
and beyond explanation
because it is too close to be explained.

Thomas Merton, *The Monastic Journey*

The ultimate meaning and purpose of life cannot be expressed, cannot properly be thought. It is present everywhere, in everything, yet it always escapes our grasp. It is the ground of all existence, that from which all things come, to which all things return, but which never appears. It is 'within' all things, 'above' all things, 'beyond' all things, but it cannot be identified with anything. Without it nothing could exist, without it nothing can be known. It is 'unseen but seeing, unheard but hearing, unperceived but perceiving, unknown but knowing' . . . We speak of 'God', but this also is only a name for this inexpressible mystery.

Bede Griffiths, *Return to the Centre*,

8

Gift

Ours is a generous God who from the start of creation has poured out an abundance of gifts and blessings, of every sort and kind, upon the world that he has made. This is one of Thomas Traherne's favourite themes and he is continually reminding us that God does not hoard but shares, extravagantly, the measure of an overflowing love which is the essence of his person:

> Bounty follows the Nature of God
> as Light doth the sun.
> Being therefore infinitly Bountifull
> He is infinitly willing to Give all Things.

He can never forget this, this world as the 'beginning of Gifts', and it comes like a refrain time and again:

> Be sensible of your Treasures.

> How Rich is the world,
> wherin I have Such possessions.

God's generosity comes from his love:

> He hath infinitly Loved us in Giving us His Works:
> infinitly Loved us in Giving us his Laws;
> in Giving us himselfe;
> in Giving us his Son;
> in Giving us our Selves.[1]

ⲥⲉⲭⲁⳍ

We find the same theme in a contemporary American who writes of the generosity of God in his terms: 'God is the first source, the prime mover and the most lavish giver of all these gifts.' The theme of this book by William Countryman is forgiveness, but he here sets it in the wider context of the many gifts of God:

> *Gift* is the principle on which the Creator has based human existence; it is the most pervasive, even if little noticed, reality of our lives. We have life itself by others' gift of procreation, pregnancy and childbirth. We are sustained in life by the good things of nature and by the labour, generosity and society of other human beings. We are educated by the self-giving of our teachers. We are sustained constantly by gifts – love, forgiveness, reconciliation, pleasure. Our whole life is a fabrication of gifts received, and we ourselves contribute our gifts to the lives of others.[2]

A seventeenth-century Anglican mystical poet, a twenty-first century Californian theologian, and now, for my third example I turn to the Celtic world where they understand this so naturally because of their own very strong tradition of hospitality. The eighth-century monastic poet Blathmac even calls God a *hospitaller* who lavishes good things on all who come:

> He is the most generous that exists:
> he is a hospitaller in possessions;
> his is every flock that he sees,
> his the wild beasts and the tame . . .
>
> To your son is sung our constant hymn,
>   his praises at every hour;
> 'Holy, holy, holy, pure is the Lord God of hosts.'[3]

ⲥⲉⲭⲁⳍ

We cannot therefore simply be receptive, although as Traherne so nicely tells us one of God's gifts is 'in makeing us to receive in the most perfect Manner', and we are to receive all these treasures in order that we may ourselves become a treasure. All these good things are meant for sharing; they remind us that we are caught up in a movement of giving and receiving, and that of course brings us back to the response of gratitude and thanks-giving, and the pattern of daily praise into which we should rightly be caught up.

For when we respond with thanks, a bond is thereby created between the giver and the one who receives: we become the thanks-giver. The practice of thanks-giving was one that children in the Outer Hebrides in the nineteenth century were taught by their mothers, just as they themselves had received it in their turn through oral tradition down countless generations. So each day would start with a great act of cosmic thanksgiving, in which they joined their human voices with those of the birds and the wild creatures in a chorus of gratitude and praise, thanking God for these daily gifts and blessings which he showered on them so 'gently and generously':

> Each thing I have received, from Thee it came,
> Each thing for which I hope, from Thy love it will come
> Each thing I enjoy, it is of Thy bounty.
>
> . . .
>
> Each day may I remember the source of the mercies
> Thou has bestowed on me gently and generously;
> Each day may I be fuller in love to Thyself.[4]

On the seventh day God rested, and rejoiced in the world that he had made, and he saw that it was good. He blessed the Sabbath and made it a day of blessing, just as he had blessed the creatures and then the humans, and had given the promise: 'The Lord will bless you.' But then we read this command in the book of Deuteronomy: 'You shall bless the Lord.' Blessing is thus a reciprocal act – we are blessed by God and we bless God in return. For when we bless, we acknowledge God as the source of our life and welfare, the origin of all goodness and gifts, and this prevents us from taking it for granted.

At the age of ninety-three, the cellist Pablo Casals explained how, for the past eighty years, he had started the day in the same manner. He went to the piano and he played two preludes and fugues of Bach: 'It is a sort of benediction on the house. But that is not its only meaning . . . It is rediscovery of the world in which I have a joy of being a part. It fills me with awareness of the wonder of life, with a feeling of the incredible marvel of being human.'[5]

ᆭ

Thanksgiving has always held a central place in both the Hebrew and the Christian traditions, and on this day I add my voice to the great paeon of praise and rejoicing which stretches down the ages and has been shared by all times and peoples.

Three times a day a Jew will praise God

> for thy miracles
> which are daily with us,
> and for thy
> continual marvels.

Praise takes a splendid form in this Jewish memorial prayer:

> Magnified and sanctified be the great name of God
> in the world which he created according to his will.
> May he establish his kingdom in your life and in your
> days,
> and in the lifetime of all his people:
> quickly and speedily may it come, and let us say
> Amen!

Blessed be God for ever!

> Blessed, praised and glorified,
> exalted, extolled and honoured,
> magnified and lauded be the name of the
>   Holy One;
> blessed be God!
> Though he be high above all the blessings
>   and hymns,
> which are uttered in the world; let us say
>   Amen!
> Blessed be God for ever![6]

༺✤༻

The vigour of the language has much in common with that of the *Altus Prosator*, the hymn traditionally attributed to St Columba, which towards its end has this glorious outpouring as we look forward to the time of rejoicing in heaven:

> By the singing of hymns eagerly ringing out,
> by thousands of angels rejoicing in holy dances,
> and by the four living creatures full of eyes,
> with the twenty-four joyful elders
> casting their crowns under the feet of the Lamb
>   of God,
> the Trinity is praised in eternal threefold
>   exchanges.[7]

'Let us sing!' 'Let us praise!' These early monastic hymns, which were sung from side to side across the choir as a choral recitation, were like a conversation – in song – between the brothers as they exchanged a narration of the wonderful things that God had done for them and in which they rejoiced. It becomes a chorus of mutual exhortation which comes not only from the community of the living but also from the community of the dead, the saints, ancestors, all those who have died, and not least the angelic hosts who are no less a part of this rejoicing community:

> Blessing and brightness,
> Wisdom, thanksgiving,
> Great power and might
> To the King who rules over all.
>
> Glory and honour and goodwill,
> Praise and the sublime song of minstrels,
> Overflowing love from every heart
> To the King of Heaven and Earth
> To the chosen Trinity has been joined
> Before all, after all, universal
> Blessing and everlasting blessing,
> Blessing everlasting and blessing.[8]

Praise comes naturally to the monastic tradition whose life and worship were shaped by the daily recitation of the Psalter. This was as true in the Egyptian desert as it was of the Celtic monks and hermits, and as it is today in any Benedictine or Cistercian community. Thomas Merton called the psalms the greatest of all religious poems:

> In the psalms we drink divine praise
> at its pure and stainless source,
> in all its primitive sincerity and perfection . . .
> If we have no real interest in praising God
> it shows that we have never realized who He is.
> For when one becomes conscious of who God really is,
> and when one realizes that He who is Almighty,
> and infinitely Holy,
> has done great things for us . . .
> the only possible reaction
> is the cry of half-articulated exultation
> that bursts from the depths of our being

in amazement
at the tremendous, inexplicable goodness
of God to men and women.[9]

Knowing the psalms by heart meant inevitably that there was an overlap between their own inner processes and the thought of the psalms. 'Semper in ore psalmus', his mouth was always filled with psalms, was a familiar *bon mot* used to describe these early monks. In the end the psalms are poetry, praise poetry and in the end monastic life is a life of praise. For even though many psalms do not hesitate to grumble and to curse God, at some point there comes this exclamation, 'But thou O God . . .' and they turn to praise a God who is not only the creator of his people, but who stands by them, who supports, leads and rescues them.

In a Benedictine community the day will start with Psalm 95:

Come ring out our joy to the Lord;
hail the God who saves us.
Let us come before him, giving thanks,
with songs let us hail the Lord.

And each day will also include Psalm 150 which rings out with a succession of Alleluias, until those final words, which of course also bring the entire Psalter to an end, the triumphant shout:

Let everything that has breath praise the Lord;
O praise the Lord! Alleluia!

Praise runs like a thread through the psalms, sometimes cosmic, sometimes personal, addressed to every human situation and experience, the words varying, the intention the same:

I will give you thanks O Lord with my whole heart.

I will rejoice and be glad in you.

I will exalt you O Lord
for you have drawn me up from the depths.

> I will bless the Lord continually:
> his praise shall be always in my mouth.
>
> Bless the Lord O my soul:
> O Lord my God how great you are!

Sometimes praise is in the context of song and dance:

> Give the Lord thanks upon the harp;
> and sing his praise to the lute of ten strings.
>
> O sing him a new song:
> make sweetest melody with shouts of praise.
>
> Praise him with the timbrel and dances:
> praise him upon the lute and harp.

Sometimes praise comes at the end of a time of sadness:

> You have turned my lamentation into dancing:
> you have put off my sackcloth and girded me with joy,
>
> that my heart may sing your praise and ever be silent:
> O Lord my God I will give you thanks for ever.

The totality of praise!

> Praise the Lord.
> Praise the Lord O my soul:
> while I live I will praise the Lord;
>
> while I have any being:
> I will sing praise to my God.
>
> Praise the Lord all his works
> in all places of his dominion.

It is not always easy to praise. Praise sometimes comes out of a desperate situation, it comes with a struggle. There are these lines of Rilke:

> O tell me, poet, what do you do? – I praise.
> But how can you endure to meet the gaze
> Of deathly and of monstrous things? – I praise.

In the week after 11 September 2001, the *New Yorker* carried a poem with the significant title 'Try to Praise the Mutilated World'. In it the Polish poet Adam Zagajewski has a refrain: 'Try to praise'; then he says you must praise; you should praise, until finally comes the simple command 'Praise'. Each time it is still the same mutilated world, but the poet searches out the moments of stillness, of beauty, of goodness, of those often fleeting and transitory gifts that we must not forget:

> Remember June's long days,
> and wild strawberries, drops of wine, the dew . . .
> and the gray feather a thrush lost,
> and the gentle light that strays and vanishes
> and returns.

❧

When we fail in wonder we fail in gratitude. The response to wonder is calling attention to the world in order to praise it.

> And the seeing will be praise
> To God as ever.[10]

The contemporary Welsh poet James Nicholas is making the connection between seeing and praising. So much of this retreat has been about seeing, seeing with wonder and delight, recovering the eyes to see and so to praise. It is something that comes into a novel by Isabel Colegate in which we are shown an ambitious, hard-headed sister who has never understood her brother or approved of him. When she would ask him what he was doing he replied that he was just looking, and it had always irritated her. One day, however, she discovers the amazing range of photographs in his attic, and as she stands in front of her brother's twenty-five years of work, she begins to see light as he had seen it – just light on darkness, or on lesser light, or against a shadowed wall, light coming from below, evening light, early morning light. And she finally understands that what she is seeing is *his solitary cry of praise.*

> The pictures implied no judgements Edith thought. Perhaps the people, incidents, objects, mountains, trees were incidental and the camera's only love affair was with the light . . . the crowds so lit had seldom an obvious reason for their having gathered. Sometimes they looked like defeated armies, sometimes like a multitude coming together praising God. Praise was certainly there, as if the consciousness behind the camera had had only one reaction to beauty and ugliness, joy, pain, error, tragedy: simply praise. This had been Alfred's life, Edith thought, moved; day after day, his solitary cry of praise had risen into the indifferent air. His vision was not hers but she understood its fierce coherence.[11]

ॐ

The word 'to bless' is in Latin *beatus*, meaning to be fortunate or happy but even more significantly, remaining close to God. So giving blessing should spill over into life and bring it a joyous fullness. As we look at these praise-prayers they help to show us 'how to be joyful, to be able to sing and dance, to celebrate beauty and goodness in circumstances of deprivation, oppression and infamy that we too can raised to new life, to be in Christ'.[12]

When I am fully alive I look around me with eyes that are open, astonished, and ears that are attentive, and as a result I experience all of life as gift. This is simply the logical conclusion of everything that I have been exploring: to see the world as gift and to respond with gratefulness – indeed Brother David Stendl-Rast says that being grateful leads into a life of fullness,

and his book *Gratefulness, the Heart of Prayer,* carries the sub-title
An Approach to Life in Fullness.[13]

❦

Is there a danger of my prayer becoming lifeless and routine?
Could God even sometimes get bored with the way I pray? A
time of retreat like this is a chance to ask myself that question.
In the Celtic world it was impossible to separate praying and
singing. Prayers and blessings were songs and poems which were
characterized by a particular lightness and joyousness. As Alex-
ander Carmichael travelled round the highlands and islands of
Scotland, the people trusted him not only with their blessings
but also told him how they prayed and sang them. How dull most
of our private praying seems compared, for example, with that of
Mary Macrae. She had been a great dancer and singer when she was
young and even when music-making had been condemned by a
Calvinistic church, she found it completely natural to continue

> singing her songs and ballads, intoning her hymns and incan-
> tations, and chanting her own mouth-music, and dancing to
> her own shadow when nothing better was available.

If before this retreat ends I were to dance my prayer I wonder
what difference it would make?

❦

Dancing needs energy, movement; if we are going to dance we
cannot sit about or lie around in some lazy, slumped position.
When so much spirituality is about being still, and that has of
course been an important element running through this retreat,
it is also important to think about energy – the right sort of
energy. The Irish theologian Donall Dorr says that if we are to
look for one word which describes the effect that Christ had on
his friends it should be 'energize'. Men and women were drawn

by the power of Christ's words and the magnetism of his dynamic
character. He held out hope and promise to those who were tired
or had lost a sense of direction, to those who felt themselves
pushed to the edge, and he challenged those who made excuses
or were cautious or half-hearted. I find the same energy and
excitement in St Benedict, and I suspect that that was one of the
things that drew people to him in his lifetime, as we today are
also still drawn by his vision – a man on fire with his love of
Christ, who was himself fully alive, and wanted other men and
women to live life to its fullest and freest.

⟨❈⟩

St Augustine writes of the totality of praise, and how it is always
new, a new song, for those who have learned to 'love a new life have
also learned to sing a new song'. So he tells us, in words that dance
with energy, that as we march on we are to sing joyful Alleluias:

> A song is a thing of joy,
> and, if we think carefully about it,
> a thing of love.
> So the man who has learned to love a new life
> has learned to sing a new song . . .
> 'But I do sing' you may reply.
> You sing, of course you sing.
> I can hear you;
> but make sure that your life
> sings the same tune as your mouth.
> Sing with your voices,
> sing with your hearts,
> sing with your lips,
> sing with your lives . . .
> Are you looking for praises to sing?
> The singer himself is the praise contained in the
> song.[14]

Prayers and Reflections

We have been fortunate in our days,
and in the places where we have lived.
To no one else belongs the praise,
but to you, the great Giver of gifts.

. . .

You will show us the path of life,
in your countenance is the fulness of joy.
From the the spring of your heart flow rivers of
delight,
a fountain of water that shall never run dry.

Psalm 16

You are a child of God . . .

We were born to make manifest
the glory of God
that is within us.
It's not just in some of us
it's within everyone.
And as we let our light shine
We unconsciously give other people
permission to do the same.
As we are liberated from our own fear
our presence automatically liberates others.

Nelson Mandela

The whole world is full of glory:

Here is the glory of created things,
　　the earth and the sky,
　　　　the sun and the moon,
　　　　　　the stars and the vast expanses:

Here is fellowship
　　with all that was created,
　　　　the air and the wind,
　　　　　　cloud and rain,
　　　　　　　　sunshine and snow:

All life like the bubbling of a flowing river
　　and the dark currents of the depths of the sea
　　is full of glory.

*

The white waves of the breath of peace
　　on the mountains,
　　　　and the light striding
　　　　　　in the distances of the sea:

The explosion of the dawn wood-pigeons
　　and the fire of the sunset doves,
　　　　sheep and cattle at their grazing,
　　　　　　the joy of countless creeping things
　　　　　　as they blossom,
　　　　　　　　spider and ant
　　　　　　　　　　of nimble disposition
　　　　　　　　　　　　proclaim the riches of goodness.

　　　　　　　　　　　　　　　Euros Bowen

In rare moments
when I am home to myself,
my heart is still,
my pulse a psalm,
I know obscurely
I receive my life
from a power beyond me,
live by a life not my own.

This morsel of life
its ephemeral beauty,
its searing sorrow,
is on loan,
marginal to a greater agency
that always, all ways
engages the darkness,
brings life from death.

My own gratuitousness
itself is gift,
liberating me
to live in this moment,
to be at peace in a world
that, like me, is passing away,
to love it fiercely,
to let it go.

Bonnie Thurston

I looked for a while at the daffodils, and asked myself the
question: What do you want of your life? and I realized, with
a start of recognition and terror 'Exactly what I have' – but
to be commensurate, to handle it all better.

9

Epilogue

> God does not die on the day when we cease to believe in a
> personal deity, but we die on the day when our lives cease
> to be illuminated by the steady radiance, renewed daily, of a
> wonder, the source of which is beyond all reason.[1]

These words, which are taken from Dag Hammarskjöld's *Markings*, were quoted during a retreat given by Michael Mayne at
Tymawr, the convent which came to mean so much to Philip
Toynbee. They express marvellously well what I have been trying
to explore in this book, and I find that this retreat, given after I
had myself finished writing, expresses clearly and forcefully what
I myself have come to believe is vital for any of us – whether
struggling on the margins of the Church, or firmly established in
our faith; whether over-worked or feeling that life seems empty:

> People often think that the basic command of religion is 'Do
> this'! or 'Don't do that!'. It isn't. It's look and wonder! learn
> to give attention to the world around you.

Wonder and attention go together. Wonder begins with giving
rapt attention to what is immediately in front of us. It is what
we learn from small children and it is a great gift for many of us
that grandchildren come into our lives when we have more time
to give them than we had when bringing up our own children,
so that we can listen to them, enjoy them and have the chance
to see the world again through their eyes. This is the eye of

innocence which can reveal simple yet profound truths. When the Revd Francis Kilvert tells us how on Easter morning, 16 April 1876, he rose early and went out into the fields of his small country parish on the Welsh Borders, he also shows us how he saw with love and joy the inter-connectedness of earth and heaven and the risen Christ. The grass was still white with hoar frost but the sky was a pure unclouded blue. The day was bright, sunny, quiet, empty. He listened to the rising of the lark and 'then came the echo and answer of earth' as the Easter bells rang out their peals from the church tower all around.

> 'The Lord is risen' smiled the sun, 'The Lord is risen' sang the lark. And the church bells in their joyous pealing answered from tower to tower 'He is risen indeed'.

Attention, wonder are close to mystery – what Bishop John V. Taylor used to call 'the sense of beyondness at the heart of things'. For this is not just seeing, it is seeing beyond. This is seeing with the eyes of the heart. It was said both of the Celtic hermits and of Thomas Merton that they saw the world 'with rinsed eyes', but it could equally well be true – or become true – of any of us.

In the *Little Prince* Saint-Exupéry wrote:

> What they (men and women) are seeking may be found in a single rose or a drop of water ... but the eyes are blind: one must seek with the heart.[2]

A drop of water for Saint-Exupéry, a grain of sand for William Blake, a hazel-nut for Julian of Norwich – and for Thomas Traherne, a common and ordinary fly. Looking at it enthroned on a green leaf, which he described as 'having a pavement of living Emerald beneath its feet, there contemplating all the World', he loved it for the curious symmetry of all its parts:

> The Infinit Workmanship about his Body,
> the Marvellous Consistence of his Lims,
> the neat & exquisit Distinction of his Joynts.

He saw it as 'a Treasure wherein all Wonders were shut up together, and that God had done as much in little there, as he had done at large in the whole World'.

Traherne saw with an *astonished* eye, with a fully awakened mind, but also with a heart of love. He looks on an apple, an ear of corn, 'an Herb', a drop of water, and finds a precious jewel – and then asks:

> Who can luv any Thing that God made too much? His infinit Goodness and Wisdom and Power and Glory are in it. What a World would this be, were every thing Beloved as it ought to be!

For Thomas Traherne, the passionate sense of relatedness to the physical world around him means enjoyment, happiness, everything that he summed up in his favourite word 'felicity', of which he called himself the sole heir – as is each one of us also. He feels himself surrounded, in the centre and midst of it.

> Evry Man is alone the Centre and Circumference of it. It is all his own, and so Glorious, that it is Eternal and Incomprehensible Essence of the Deitie.[3]

And his response?

> And evry thing he sees, his Ey
> Does Bless & Magifie.

There is one passage in which Traherne gives lyrical expression to this, which lies at the heart of his vision, of his prayer, of his religious faith – they cannot be separated. It is very familiar and must be the most frequently quoted of all Traherne's writing, but I still turn to it again here for it is a passage of which I never tire. I hope that breaking up the prose and setting it out in the form of a prose poem will encourage slow reflective reading:

> You never Enjoy the World aright,
> till the Sea itself floweth in your Veins,
> till you are clothed with the Heavens,

and Crowned with the Stars:
and perceive yourself to be
the Sole Heir of the whole world:
and more than so,
because Men are in it
who are evry one Sole Heirs,
as well as you.

Yet further, you never Enjoy the World aright,
till you so lov the Beauty of Enjoying it,
that you are Covetous and Earnest
to persuade others to Enjoy it . . .
The World is a Mirror of infinite Beauty,
yet no man regard it.
It is a Region of Light and Peace,
did not Men Disquiet it.[4]

And as Traherne takes us from seeing to loving, so too does Michael Mayne:

I guess that, in the end, the giving of proper attention to what lies all about us and within us, and to whoever or whatever is before our eyes, is much more than the beginning of wonder. For it's also a pretty good definition of love. And therefore it is also the surest, swiftest way to God, who is both our journey and our journey's end.

❦

As I have lived, read and prayed myself through the writing of this book I have turned with delight to the many people who have opened my eyes and enriched my own life, and I hope that the words that I have quoted and wanted to share will become a source of prayer and insight for all who read it. Coming from different eras and different backgrounds, they have one thing in common: they are showing us how they themselves lived, and saw their world, and loved and rejoiced. They show us that this too is how any of us can also live, if we so choose. But it does ask of us that we quite deliberately take upon ourselves this task, this responsibility, of seeing rather than looking, of seeing into and seeing beyond. It is all part of that fullness of life that a generous God would wish for all of us.

The promise of where the journey of life might take us is expressed nowhere more brilliantly than in the ending of *King Lear*:

> So we'll live,
> And pray, and sing, and tell old tales, and laugh
> At gilded butterflies . . .
> And take upon's the mystery of things,
> As if we were God's spies.[5]

Will I, or will I not, take upon myself this task, this supreme task, as Helen Luke describes it when she tells us that it is the final responsibility of each person's life?

For we are given this opportunity to become as it were *God's spy*. This was an image that was lost on me when in earlier years I used so often to stand in front of Redemption window, placed in the furthermost eastern chapel of Canterbury cathedral by its Benedictine monastic community in the thirteenth century. The succession of panels tell the story of our human redemption, God's saving grace at work in the history of Israel and in Christ's earthly life. Jewel-like stained glass draws the eye up to Christ in majesty, the pantocrator, seated on an orb, his right hand upheld in blessing, *Solus ab eterno creo cuncta creata guberno*, alone from eternity I create all things and govern creation. But the very lowest panel of all shows us two spies, carrying between them a rod from which hands a huge bunch of grapes. One turns away, the other does not. The pleasure in an image is the way in which one can uncover layers of meanings, and find connections which show new levels of meaning. Now I see two men exploring a new country, trying to discover what it has to offer. A spy looks on each thing with an urgent eye, letting no detail escape, searching under every stone, on the look-out not simply for treasure but ready to unearth the hidden and the mysterious.

And so I have chosen to end with words taken from Helen Luke since they express what I feel, that there can be no ending here, no goal, no conclusion, but simply an encouragement to penetrate deeper and deeper into the gift of being placed in a world of mystery, wonder, delight.

> A spy is one who penetrates a hidden mystery,
> and a spy of God
> is one who sees at the heart
> of every manifestation of life
> the *mysterium tremendum* that is God.[6]

> Flame-dancing Spirit, come,
> Sweep us off our feet and
> Dance us through our days.
> Surprise us with your rhythms,
> Dare us to try new steps, explore
> New patterns and new partnerships.
> Release us from old routines,
> To swing in abandoned joy
> And fearful adventure.
> And in the intervals,
> Rest us,
> In your still centre.

Ann Lewin, Candles & Kingfishers

Notes

1 The Starting Point

1. Ralph Harper, *On Presence, Variations and Reflections*, Philadelphia: Trinity Press International, 1991, pp. 93–4.

2. I read this first in *Holiness*, London: Darton, Longman & Todd, 1981, and have been grateful ever since, and even though I forget it time and again I recall it as a point of reference to how ideally I should treat food.

3. I have quoted the text here from the new translation by Patrick Barry OSB, *Saint Benedict's Rule, A new translation for today*, Ampleforth Abbey Press, 1997 together with the commentary by Terrence G. Kardong, *Benedict's Rule, A Translation and Commentary*, Collegeville, Minnesota: The Liturgical Press, 1996, p. 11.

4. I am quoting Catherine Wybourne OSB, 'Seeing by the light that comes from God', *Benedictines*, Winter 1998, LI.2, p. 21, a periodical published by Mount St Scholastica, Atchison, Kansas.

5. For those who do not already possess one, magnifying glasses can generally be found in any good chemist's shop. A small one, magnification of ten, is quite sufficient.

6. These lines are taken from his 'Ode to Things', *Neruda's Garden, An Anthology of Odes*, selected and translated by Maria Jacketti, Pittsburgh, Penn.: Latin American Library Review Press, 1995, pp. 227–33.

7. Susan Stevenot Sullivan ' "How can this be?", The New Mystery of Monastic Vocation', *Benedictines*, Winter 1999, LII.2, pp. 26–31.

8. I owe this phrase to the Revd Canon Paul Iles, who as Precentor of Hereford Cathedral gave a series of Lenten talks in which he used the image of the cloister as a means of exploring the many ways in which prayer can develop.

9. *Letter* 1.xv. I owe this quotation to Charles Dumont OCSO, *Praying*

the Word of God, the use of lectio divina, Fairacres, Oxford: SLG Press, Convent of the Incarnation, 1999, p. 1.

10. An excellent short introduction is that of Charles Dumont referred to above. For a fuller treatment see Michael Casey, *The Art of Sacred Reading*, Australia, Dove: Harper Collins, 1995. Martin L. Smith, *The Word is Very Near You, A Guide to Praying with Scripture*, Cambridge, Mass.: Cowley Publications, 1989, puts it into a wider context and is extremely clear and useful. Norvene Vest, Benedictine oblate provides a simple and practical approach in *No Moment too Small, Rhythms of Silence, Prayer and Holy Reading*, Kalamazoo, Michigan: Cistercian Publications, 1994.

11. See Mick Hales, *Monastic Gardens*, Stewart, Tabori and Chang, 2001, ch. 1, 'The Cloister Garth'. This is a magnificently illustrated book which is itself virtually an exercise in contemplation.

12. St Ambrose, treatise *On Cain and Abel*, Book 1, 9, 34–9. The full text from which I have taken the extract comes in the readings for Monday of Week 27 in the *Divine Office*, according to the Roman Rite.

13. This is taken from Martin Smith SSJE when he was superior of the Cowley Fathers writing about one of his brothers in America in *Nativities and Passions, Words for Transformation*, London: Darton, Longman & Todd, 1996, p. 39, Boston, Mass.: Cowley Publications, 1995.

14. *The Genesee Diary* now appears in many editions in both America and England. I have taken my quotations from Sunday 22 December and from the Conclusion. The Diary was originally published in 1976.

2 Seeing with the Inner Eye

1. This is taken from the brochure of the Oxford Summer School Conference 2001 hosted by Wycliffe Hall in collaboration with Regent College, Vancouver, 'Capturing the Imagination', presided over by Trevor Hart, Director of the Institute for Theology, Imagination and the Arts.

2. As so often, Merton has proved to be prophetic. This was written in *Contemplation in a World of Action* published posthumously in 1973 and recent years have shown how true his words were. More and more attention is being paid to the role of poetry and the imagination. It is now many years since Urban Holmes wrote *Ministry and the Imagination*, in which he said how crucial the imagination was in hearing God's word – above all in times of crisis. Today there are increasing numbers of books of contemporary religious poetry and new editions of earlier poets,

such as the seventeenth-century English mystical figures George Herbert, John Donne, Thomas Traherne and Henry Vaughan. Books are being published with titles such as *The Poetic Imagination, An Anglican Spiritual Tradition* (by L. William Countryman, London: Darton, Longman & Todd, New York, Orbis 1999). I also want to mention in passing that my own study of *The Celtic Way of Prayer*, originally published in England in 1996, re-issued in 2003 by Hodder & Stoughton, and in America in 1997, by Doubleday, New York, carries the sub-title *The Recovery of the Religious Imagination*.

3. *The Habit of Being, Letters of Flannery O'Connor*, ed. Sally Fitzgerald, New York: Vintage Books, 1980, p. 70.

4. Ann and Barry Ulanov, *The Healing Imagination, the Meeting of Psyche and Soul*, Integration Books, 1991, pp. 14–15.

5. See Rowan Williams, 'New Words for God, Contemplation and Religious Writing', in Thomas Merton, *Poet, Monk, Prophet, Papers presented to the Thomas Merton Society Conference at Oakham School 1998*, Abergavenny: Three Peaks Press, 1998, pp. 39–48.

5. This comes from a talk given at Bleddfa, a centre in the Welsh Borders established by James Roose-Evans.

6. I owe this to Jim Forest in a talk 'Thomas Merton and the Christ of the Byzantine Icons', given in Winchester, England 10 December 1993 for a Merton Celebration. Merton's Timex watch was valued at $10; the value of his dark glasses, his breviary, his rosary (broken) and the icon were all nil.

7. This is taken from the Foreword written by Bishop Kallistos Ware to the book by Rowan Williams, *Ponder These Things, Praying with Icons of the Virgin*, Norwich: The Canterbury Press, 2002, and all that follows owes much to that simple but profound study.

8. Edwin Muir, 'The Annunciation'. I owe this poem and the comment to Melvyn Matthews *Delighting in God*, London: Collins, Fount, 1987, pp. 26–7.

9. Rowan Williams, *After Silent Centuries*, Oxford: The Perpetua Press, 1984, p. 11.

10. In Andrew Motion we have an English Poet Laureate who is trying to make poetry more generally accessible and this comes from a broadcast on national poetry day in England in 2000.

11. This comes from a talk at the American Benedictine Academy Convention 1993, *Creating a Renewed Monastic Environment*, which was concerned with 'the challenge to enter more deeply and intuitively into the symbolic level of our identity'.

12. Mark Oakley, *The Collage of God*, London: Darton, Longman & Todd, 2001, p. 43.

13. Roger Housden, *Ten Poems to Change your Life*, New York: Harmony Books, 2001, in his introduction, pp. 1–7.

14. Mark Oakley is here quoting the Australian poet Les Murray who maintains that a church responsive to its poetic vocation will be watchful of its words and their patterning and crafting: *The Collage of God*, pp. 46–7, and footnote 40.

15. Merton's talks were recorded so that the larger community could share in his teachings. They have since been recorded and made more generally available by Credence Cassettes, P. O. Box 419491, Kansas City, MO 64141 6491.

16. 'Ode to Things', *Neruda's Garden, An Anthology of Odes*, selected and translated by Maria Jackett, Pittsburgh, Penn.: Latin American Literary Review Press, 1995, pp. 227–33.

17. Mark Oakley, *Spiritual Society, Secular Church? Private Prayer and Public Religion*, the Seventeenth Eric Symes Abbott Memorial Lecture given in Westminster Abbey, Spring 2002, p. 6.

18. William Johnston, *Mirror of the Mind*, London: Collins, Fount, 1981 p. 14.

19. Rainer Maria Rilke, *Letters to a Young Poet*, New York: Norton, 1954, pp. 34–5.

20. A. M. Allchin, *Praise Above All, Discovering the Welsh Tradition*, Cardiff: University of Wales Press, 1991, pp. 42–3.

3 Silence

1. David Arfam, 'Freeze Frame', an article in the *Journal of the Royal Academy*, 2000.

2. James Finley, *Merton's Palace of Nowhere, A Search for God through Awareness of the True Self*, Notre Dame, Ind.: Ave Maria Press, 1978 p.117.

3. *Day of a Stranger* in *A Thomas Merton Reader*, ed. P. McDonnell, New York: Image Books, 1974, London: Lamp Press, 1989, p. 436.

4. June Boyce-Tillman, *The Creative Spirit, Harmonious Living with Hildegard of Bingen*, Norwich: The Canterbury Press, 2000, pp. 185–6.

5. *Writings from the Philokalia on Prayer of the Heart*, translated by E. Kadloubovsky and G. E. H. Palmer, London: Faber & Faber, 1951. The Foreword, written on Mount Athos, explains that this is a collection of Greek texts, the writings of the Fathers, giving guiding instructions and

helpful advice on the way to awaken attention and consciousness, and to develop them, since the obstacles are numberless and multiform and these writings will define those difficulties and tell us how to vanquish and master them.

6. This appears on the opening page of *The Seven Storey Mountain*, originally published in New York by Harcourt, Brace and Company in 1948 and subsequently reissued in numerous editions. It first appeared in England edited by Evelyn Waugh who made it more acceptable to an English readership by omitting the uncomplimentary things that Merton said about his time in Cambridge. *Elected Silence, The Autobiography of Thomas Merton*, London: Hollis and Carter, 1949.

7. *Silence in Heaven, A book of the Monastic Life, text by Thomas Merton, with 90 photographs and texts from religious writings*, London: Thames & Hudson, 1955, p. 23.

8. All these quotations are taken from *Silence in Heaven*, quoted above.

9. See also Eugene Stockton, *Wonder a Way to God*, Australia: St Paul's, 1998.

10. *Contemplative Prayer*, New York: Doubleday, 1971, p. 90.

11. David Tomlins, 'The Meaning and Value of Silence in Christian Living', *Cistercian Studies*, XVII, 1982: 2, pp. 173, 175.

12. Mary Margaret Funk, *Tools Matter for Practising the Spiritual Life*, New York and London: Continuum, 2001. See especially the sections on guarding the heart and watchfulness of thoughts, pp. 52–6.

13. James Finley, *Merton's Palace of Nowhere, A Search for God through Awareness of the True Self*, Notre Dame, Ind.: Ave Maria Press, 1978, p. 126.

14. Sermon 99.2. See *A Gathering of Friends, The Learning and Spirituality of John of Forde*, ed. Hilary Costello and Christopher Holdsworth, Kalamazoo, Michigan: Cistercian Publications, 1996, p. 192.

15. From the homilies given at the funeral rites of Cardinal George Basil Hume, Archbishop of Westminster, published by Westminster Cathedral, London, 1999.

16. This is taken from an article that she wrote in the *Listener* on 7 March 1992 as part of a series, 'How I Pray'.

4 Attention

1. John V. Taylor, *A Matter of Life and Death*, London, SCM Press, 1986, p. 7. Many of us are grateful for a succession of seminal books

which came from the pen of John Taylor, in particular, *The Primal Vision, Christian Presence amid African Religion*, first published 1963 and reissued by SCM Press in 2001 and *Enough is Enough*, SCM Press, 1975. He also published in 1989 the poems that he always sent to friends at Christmas, *A Christmas Sequence and Other Poems*, Oxford: The Amate Press, 1989, in which he explained that the motive behind this was that 'of recapturing for an instant a child's unique astonishment'.

2. Thomas Merton, *New Seeds of Contemplation*, New York: Doubleday, 1966, p. 29.

3. Mary Oliver, *Winter Hours, Prose, Prose Poems, and Poems*, Boston, New York: Houghton Mifflin, 1999, pp. 98–100.

4. Michael Cardew, *A Pioneer Potter: An Autobiography*, London: Collins, 1988, p. 89.

5. Ruth Bidgood, 'Flying Kites', originally appeared in *Lighting Candles* 1989, and is included in *Selected Poems*, Seren Books, Bridgend, Wales, 1992, p. 105.

6. P. J. Kavanagh, see *A Kind of Journal*, Manchester, Carcanet, 2003.

7. Sr Macrine Wiederkehr, *A Tree Full of Angels, Seeing the Holy in the Ordinary*, San Francisco: Harper & Row, 1988, p. 11.

8. Mary Morrison, *Let Evening Come, Reflections on Ageing*, New York: Bantam Books, 1998, p. 74.

9. Philip Simmons, *Learning to Fall, The Blessings of an Imperfect Life*, New York: Bantam Books, 2002. The quotation comes on p. 145 but I have in fact taken it from a review of the book in *Spiritus, Journal of Christian Spirituality*, Vol. 2, No. 2, Fall 2002, pp. 243–4.

10. A. J. Heschel, *Man is Not Alone: A Philosophy of Religion*, New York: Farrar, Strauss & Young, Inc. 1951, p. 88.

11. May Sarton, *Plant Dreaming Deep*, New York: W. W. Norton & Company Inc., 1968, p. 180.

12. May Sarton, *Journal of a Solitude*, New York: W. W. Norton & Company Inc., 1973, p. 99.

13. Philip Toynbee, *Part of a Journey: An Autobiographical Journal 1977–79*, London: Collins, Fount Paperback, 1981. The quotations start with his diary for 12 November on p. 56 and it is worth while reading on from there and seeing how his art of seeing grows and develops until at one point he is saying 'But now all I want is to look harder and see better.'

14. Ron Seitz, *Song for Nobody, A Memory Vision of Thomas Merton*, Ligouri, Missouri: Triumph Books, 1993, pp. 133–4.

15. Thomas Merton, *The Sign of Jonas*, New York: Harcourt, Brace and Co., 1953, pp. 91–2. There is an interesting parallel here with Philip Toynbee on his visits to Monmouth, the local market town, when he confesses that he used to hate shopping before but now he finds that 'ships, houses and people were all clarified in the same way. My shopping itself is now very deliberate and considered; trying to acquire grace through attention.'

16. John Howard Griffin, *A Hidden Wholeness, The Visual World of Thomas Merton*, Boston: Houghton Mifflin, 1979. My own book on Merton, *A Seven Day Journey with Thomas Merton*, includes many of his photographs. It is no longer in print in England but in America it is published by Servant Publications, Ann Arbor, Michigan, and has many of his hitherto unpublished photographs which the abbey of Gethsemani most generously made available to me when they learnt that I was anxious to use the visual as well as the verbal in Merton's work.

17. Ann Lamott, *Bird by Bird, Some Instructions on Writing and Life*, New York: Anchor, Random House, 1994, p. 98.

5 *Change*

1. *The Image of Christ*, the catalogue of the exhibition 'Seeing Salvation' published by the National Gallery, London, 2000, distributed by Yale University Press, pp. 120–1.

2. I owe these two poems, the first of which is not yet published, to my good friend Bonnie Thurston. The second is from 'Roots First, Feet First' which appeared in the journal *Presence* 7/2, California, 2002.

3. This is something written by Neville Ward but I can no longer find the reference.

4. *The Coracle* was a small pamphlet published from the late 1930s by the Iona community to which George McLeod contributed regularly. It has photographs of the work in progress as the abbey was being rebuilt, and contains many contributions which show this earliest vision of a place which has now become a mecca for the many people worldwide who have in recent years discovered Celtic spirituality.

5. Marcus Borg, *The God We Never Knew*, San Francisco: Harper, 1998.

6. John Chrysostom, *Hom.* 13, 1–2

7. Michael Casey, *Truthful Living, St Benedict's Teaching on Humility*, Petersham, Mass.: St Bede's Publications, 1999, p. 78.

8. I have used two different translations in the previous quotations. I have taken the opening lines from Terrence Kardong *Benedict's Rule. A Translation and Commentary*, Collegeville, Minnesota: The Liturgical Press, 1996, and the final lines from the translation of Patrick Barry, quoted earlier.

I owe this fascinating point about the relationship between the cantor and the choir to an article by Dom John Fortin 'The Presence of God: a Linguistic and Thematic Link between the dictatorial and liturgical section of the Rule of St Benedict', *Downside Review*, Vol. 117, no. 409, October 1999, pp. 293–309.

9. While I was in Australia I had access to the notes of the lectures that Michael Casey gave to the Good Samaritan Sisters from which this is taken. I used some of his material in what I wrote about chapter 19 in A *Life-Giving Way, A Commentary on the Rule of St Benedict*, London: Geoffrey Chapman, 1995, re-issued London: Continuum, 1998, p. 85, published in America by Collegeville, Minnesota: The Liturgical Press.

10. This is a theme which I have explored more fully in *Living with Contradiction*, Norwich: The Canterbury Press and Harrisburg; Pennsylvania: Morehouse Publications, 1997. The quotation comes from an article on the ascetical and coenobetic tradition in *Cistercian Studies*, 1976, XI, 2, p. 263.

11. See *Thomas Merton Poet, Monk, Prophet, Papers presented at the second General Conference of the Thomas Merton Society at Oakham School 1998*, Abergavenny: Three Peaks Press, 1998.

12. *Cistercian Studies Quarterly*, 32.1, 1997, is devoted almost entirely to Aelred of Rievaulx and includes a number of his sermons.

13. *The Asian Journal of Thomas Merton*, New York: New Direction Books, 1968, pp. 230–6. These pages also include very striking photographs of the figures.

14. *Woods, Shore, Desert A Notebook, May 1968*, Santa Fe: University of New Mexico Press, 1982, p. 48.

15. Philip Toynbee, *Part of a Journey. An Autobiographical Journal 1977–1979*, London: Collins, 1981, p. 139.

16. *Part of a Journey*, pp. 261–2.

17. *The Sign of Jonas*, New York: Harcourt, Brace & Company, 1953. This is one of my favourite books by Merton, and it ends with that incomparable piece of writing, 'Fire Watch'.

18. Catherine de Hueck Doherty, Strannick, *The Call to Pilgrimage for Western Man*, Notre Dame, Indiana: Ave Maria Press, 1978, pp. 44, 49.

Anyone who might be interested in reading further on this subject could
see the first chapter of my *Celtic Way of Prayer, The Recovery of the
Religious Imagination*, London: Hodder & Stoughton, new ed. 2003, New
York: Doubleday, 1997, the chapter on 'Journeying'.

19. Kathleeen Powers Erikson, *At Eternity's Gate, The Spiritual Vision
of Vincent Van Gogh*, Grand Rapids, Michigan, and Cambridge: Eerd-
man's, 1998, pp. 162–4. The first quotation is dated 5 Nov 1876.

20. Raymond Brown, *The Gospel of John* II, p. 630, which I owe to
Demetrius Dumm, *Cherish Christ Above All, The Bible in the Rule
of Benedict*, Saint Vincent Archabbey, 1996, distributed by Gracewing,
p. 47.

6 Dark and Light

1. Psalm 126.6. This is the translation taken from the *Book of Common
Prayer of the Episcopal Church in America*.

2. John W. Kiser, *The Monks of Tibhirine, Faith, Love and Terror in
Algeria*, New York: St Martin's Press, 2002, p. 51. Here is a slightly
paraphrased translation, made for me by my brother-in-law, the Revd
Dr Christopher Armstrong, which is not that to be found in this very
remarkable book which gives a profoundly moving account of this
Trappist community in Algeria.

> There are nights when I experience faith as anguish;
> There is doubt, madness too,
> In this solitary love of a God
> who is at the same time
> Absent and all absorbing.
> . . . I hope; but what I hope for is out of sight . . .
> That tortures me as I face him.
> All the torment has direction and meaning there
> Where it is hidden in God, as though coming to birth;
> JOY, yes, but wrapped in NIGHT.

3. Seamus Heaney, *Preoccupations, Selected Poetry and Prose 1968–1978*,
London: Faber & Faber 1980, p. 189.

4. Thomas Owen Clancy and Gilbert Markus, *Iona, The Earliest Poetry
of a Celtic Monastery*, Edinburgh: Edinburgh University Press, 1995, p. 1;
Kenneth Jackson, *Studies in Early Celtic Nature Poetry*, Cambridge:
Cambridge University Press, 1995 p. 105.

5. Philip Toynbee, *Part of a Journey*, p. 147.

6. Peter Levi, *Flutes of Autumn*, London: Harvill Press 1983.

7. T. S. Eliot, *The Cocktail Party, A Comedy*, London: Faber & Faber, 1950.

8. *Cry the Beloved Country, A Story of Comfort in Desolation* was first published in 1953.

9. The full text is given in my *The Celtic Way of Prayer*, new edition, London: Hodder & Stoughton, 2003, pp. 105–6, and New York: Doubleday, 1997, pp. 123–3.

10. These quotations are taken from Irenee Hausherr SJ, *Penthos, The Doctrine of Compunction in the Christian East*, Kalamazoo, Michigan: Cistercian Publications, Inc. 1982. See especially p. 55 note.

11. The American edition appears from Cowley Publications, Cambridge, Mass.

12. Irenee Hausherr, *Penthos*, p. 140.

13. *Penthos*, p. 141.

14. *Part of a Journey*, p. 313.

15. This is taken from a sermon by Austen Farrer, *Said or Sung, An arrangement of homily and verse*, London: Faith Press, 1960, p. 58. I owe this to the Revd Canon James Coutts.

16. *After Silent Centuries*, Oxford: The Perpetua Press, 1984, p. 11.

17. This final sentence comes from Maggie Ross, *The Fountain & the Furnace, The Way of Tears and Fire*, New York: Paulist Press, 1987, p. 134.

18. Harry Williams, *Some Day I'll Find You*, Mitchell Beazley, 1982, p. 177.

19. Susan Cole-King in *The Official Report of the Lambeth Conference 1998*, Harrisburg, PA: Morehouse Publishing, 1998, p. 478.

20. These paragraphs owe much to an article by Sr Irene Nowell OSB 'The Psalms: Living Water of Our Lives', *Benedictines*, Summer 1999, LII.1 pp. 22–33. She shows us how exploring the book of Psalms can be a personal formative experience of great profundity, and coming as it does out of the experience of a Benedictine woman living and praying the psalms throughout a long life we can hear her with gratitude. The quotation from Thomas Merton is from *Bread in the Wilderness*, New York: New Directions, 1953, p. 66.

21. Helen Luke, *Old Age, Journey into Simplicity*, New York: Parabola Books, 1987, pp. 103–112. The quotation given here comes on p. 109. Helen Luke was born in 1904 in London but moved to America in 1949, after studying at Oxford and London and then in Zurich because of her

interest in Jung. She founded the Apple Farm community in Michigan in 1962 and lived there until her death.

22. This is taken from the catalogue to the National Gallery exhibition *The Image of Christ*, National Gallery, London, 2000, distributed by Yale University Press, p. 196.

23. Keith Ward, *The Promise*, London: SPCK, 1980.

24. Helen Luke, *Old Age*, p. 104.

25. I owe this to John Drury, in *The Burning Bush*, London: Collins, Fount, 1990, pp. 68–9.

7 Mystery

1. Mary Oliver, *Winter Hours, Prose, Prose Poems and Poems*, Boston, New York: Mariner Books, Houghton Mifflin, 1999, p. 101.

2. I found this in Arthur Jones and Dolores Leckey, *Facing Fear in Faith*, Thomas More, an RCL company, 2002, pp. 93–4.

3. I owe this suggestive phrase to a book which I have found most refreshing: Kim Taplin, *Tongues in Trees, Studies in Literature & Ecology*, Devon: Green Books, 1989. It comes in the section where she is discussing the poetry of Frances Horowitz pp. 198–209.

4. Philip Toynbee, *Part of a Journey*, p. 259.

5. I owe much of this material to Hilary Richardson in an article 'Themes in Eriugena's writings and early Irish art', in *History and Eschatology in John Scottus Eriugena and his Time*, ed. James McEvoy and Michael Dunnem, Leuven: Leuven University Press, 2002, p. 265. Anyone interested in this subject should read further in the many articles by Hilary Richardson, and also see her chapter 'Celtic Art', in J. P. Mackey (ed.), *An Introduction to Celtic Christianity*, Edinburgh: T&T Clark, 1989.

6. Charles Hefling (ed.), Charles Williams, *Essential Writings in Spirituality and Theology*, Cambridge and Boston, Mass: Cowley Publications, 1993, from the introduction.

7. Richard Mortimer, *A Hidden Treasure Revealed, an Introduction to the Cosmati Pavement*, Westminster Abbey Occasional Papers, no. 1, 1991. See also Richard Foster, *Patterns of Thought. The Hidden Meaning of the Great Pavement of Westminster Abbey*, London: Jonathan Cape, 1991, p. 149.

Many levels of meaning came naturally to the medieval world, accustomed as they were to approaching the Bible in this way. John Cassian in the fourth century had established the four levels that were then to become so familiar. First comes the literal description of an event; next the allegorical expounds its significance in terms of Christian faith; thirdly the trologogical reveals its moral significance, and finally *anagogia*, the transcendental moves from the tangible to the hidden truth of the invisible world. This schema was also applied to the natural world, which was seen equally with Scriptures as the way in which God revealed himself and was as St Bernard declared to be read in the same way as the word of God. This paragraph owes much to Foster's interpretation, especially p. 149.

8. Richard Foster, *Patterns of Thought*, p. 130. There are a good many studies of the Book of Kells but the best short introduction is that by Peter Brown, librarian of Trinity College Dublin where it is housed. It was published by Thames & Hudson in 1980.

9. These are the words of the fourteenth-century Franciscan theologian and bishop of Lincoln Robert Grosseteste.

10. *The Asian Journal of Thomas Merton*, ed. Naomi Burton, Patrick Hart and James Laughlin from his original notebooks, New York: New Direction Books, 1968, pp. 233–6.

11. Benedicta Ward, *The Sayings of the Desert Fathers*, London: Mowbrays, 1975, p. 88.

12. I owe this to the Rev. Canon James Coutts. The full text, in the translation by Joseph P. Clancy, is to be found in the volume he edited, *Twentieth-Century Welsh Poems*, Gower Press, 1982, pp. 190–1. Two lines from this poem, again in the unpublished translation, appear again towards the end of this book.

> And the seeing will be praise
> To God as ever.

13. R. S. Thomas, *Later Poems 1972–1982*, London, Macmillan, 1983, p. 194.

14. 'A Wise Man', verses 10 and 11. This is a recently discovered manuscript in Lambeth Palace Library now published for the first time by Denise Inge, *Thomas Traherne, Poetry and Prose*, London: SPCK, 2002, p. 109.

15. There are now a number of editions of Traherne's *Centuries* and so it is best to give simply the reference to 'The First Century', section 60.

16. Philip Toynbee, *Part of a Journey*, p. 70.

17. *Part of a Journey*, p. 76.

18. *Part of a Journey*, p. 8.

19. This idea, though not the way in which it is written here, is taken from a broadcast homily, 22 September 2002, from St Paul's Covent Garden.

20. 'The Third Century', section 2.

21. This was something that I heard Bishop Kallistos Ware say during a meditation.

22. He titled his book, *The Collage of God*. See Chapter 2, 'Seeing with the Inner Eye', n. 12 above.

23. *Tertium Organum*, 1912.

24. Ben Okri, secular sermon delivered in Trinity College Cambridge in 1993.

8 Gift

1. It is difficult to give any references here – I can only recommend readers to discover Traherene to read him extravagently and give themselves up to his writings and to feel his sense of the fullness of life and our response to it.

2. William Countryman, *Forgiven and Forgiving*, Harrisburg: Morehouse, Publishing, 1998, p. 83.

3. Blathmac was an eighth-century Irish poet who retold the Biblical story in long narrative verse. His work has the interest of belonging to the movement that produced the great scriptural Irish high crosses that I mentioned earlier (pp. 123f.). For the full text see James Carney (ed.), *The Poems of Blathmac Son of Cu Brettan*, Dublin: Irish Texts Society, 1966. This is taken from stanzas 194, 198.

4. *Carmina Gadelica*, III 58–9. The full text may be found in my edition in *The Celtic Vision*, London: Darton, Longman & Todd, 1988, pp. 31–2, or in the new edition in America published by Ligouri Triumph, Ligouri, Missouri, p. 10.

5. This is taken from *Song of the Birds*, compiled by John Lloyd Webber, Robson Books, 1985. quoted by Michael Mayne in *This Sunrise of Wonder, Letters for the Journey*, London: Collins, Fount, p. 87. Many of the themes of this rich and wonderful book overlap with those that I have been exploring in this retreat and so, although it is a book to which I have returned time and again in the past, and of which I have given away numberless copies in order to share it with others, I have deliberately not referred to it while I was writing this book, with this one exception.

I hope, however, that I can encourage all those who have not yet read
it to do so at once.

6. This was used at the Thanksgiving service for Donald Coggan, the
Archbishop of Canterbury who showed such concern for the international council of Christians and Jews.

7. Thomas Owen Clancy and Gilbert Markus, *Iona, The Earliest Poetry
of a Celtic Monastery*, Edinburgh: Edinburgh University Press 1994,
pp. 52–3. This collection gives both the Latin and the English. The editors
would date this to the seventh century and tell us that it was very popular
with the medieval Church.

8. Oliver Davies and Fiona Bowie, *Celtic Christian Spirituality, Medieval
and Modern*, London: SPCK, 1995, p. 29. This is a ninth-century Old
Irish hymn of praise which is derived from the doxology found in
Revelation 7.12: 'Praise and glory and wisdom, thanksgiving and honour,
power and might, be to our God for ever and ever.'

9. Thomas Merton, *Praying the Psalms*, Collegeville, Minnesota: Liturgical Press, 1956. I have taken sentences from pages 7, 10–11, and have
set them out in this form.

10. I have already quoted from this poem by James Nicholas on p. 131.

11. Isabel Colegate, *Winter Journey*, London: Penguin Books, 1995,
pp. 194–5.

12. This particular quotation and much of the thinking about blessing
is taken from Richard J. Woods, *The Spirituality of the Celtic Saints*, New
York: Maryknoll, Orbis Books, 2000, pp. 147ff.

13. David Stendl-Rast, *Gratefulness, the Heart of Prayer*, New York:
Paulist Press, 1984.

14. Augustine, *Sermon*, 34.

9 Epilogue

1. Dag Hammarskjöld, *Markings*, London: Faber & Faber, 1966, p. 64.

2. Antoine de Saint-Exupéry, *The Little Prince*, London: William
Heineman, 1945, London: Egmont Books, 2002, p. 77.

3. Thomas Traherne, *Fifth Century*, No. 3.

4. Thomas Traherne,

5. Shakespeare, *King Lear*, Act V, Scene 3.

6. Helen Luke, *Old Age, Journey and Simplicity*, New York: Parabola
Books, 1987, p. 30.

'Fathers and Friends'
Short Biographical Sketches

This phrase was used by Thomas Merton, the twentieth-century Trappist monk – though now I am sure he would amend it to include Mothers – as he taught the young novices in the monastery at Gethsemani, sharing with them his own excitement at the riches held by the Christian tradition, above all that of the monastic men and women, both of the East and the West. I have used it to head the short biographical sketches which now follow of those whom I have quoted in the text, often only briefly, but here at least is some context in which to put them. My hope of course is that readers may be encouraged to search and to discover them for themselves, and that they will find in them a quarry for study and for prayer.

There are now many ways in which to access them. Those who use the Divine Office according to the Roman rite and say the Office of Readings are given a short daily non-scriptural reading. Another excellent collection is *A Word in Season*, *Monastic Lectionary for the Divine Office*, Villanova Pa.: Augustinian Press, a succession of volumes from 1987 onwards. I also recommend Robert Atwell's collections *Celebrating the Saints* and *Celebrating the Seasons* published by the Canterbury Press (1998 and 1999).

St Aelred of Rievaulx, 1109–1167. A native of Yorkshire who in 1133 entered the Cistercian abbey of Rievaulx, where he remained for the rest of his life and made this Yorkshire community a beacon for many hundreds of monks. He combined his pastoral activity with some of the most superb of twelfth-century writing – above all *The Mirror of Charity* and *Spiritual Friendship*.

St Ambrose, 339–397. Influenced by the Greek fathers he was Bishop of Milan and his preaching combined the two worlds.

St Athanasius, *c.* 296–373. Born in Alexandria, where he became Bishop in 328. In the controversy which raged during his lifetime he opposed the Arians and upheld the doctrine of the divinity of Christ.

St Anselm, 1033–1109. Although Italian by birth he joined the Benedictine community of Bec in Normandy where he became abbot in 1060 at the age of 27. In 1093 he most reluctantly left this valley which he loved so greatly in order to become Archbishop of Canterbury. He was a most impressive and erudite philosopher but he also had a gift for reflective and pastoral writing, and on the many occasions that I have led pilgrimages to Bec, the group of pilgrims have found inspiration in his prayers and reflections.

St Augustine, 354–430. One of the greatest and most influential of early Christian thinkers and a theologian of quite enormous range. He became the Bishop of Hippo in North Africa. Here his preaching drew great crowds, but he also found time to write, including two of the great classics of the Church: *Confessions* and *City of God*.

St Benedict, 480–540. We come to know him through his *Rule* which tells us much about the way in which he himself lived and loved Christ and wanted others to do the same. The *Rule* has inspired monastic men and woman down the centuries and today is reaching many lay people who find that that they can relate to his down to earth wisdom.

St Bernard, 1090–1153. A staggering genius of a man, larger than life, politician, administrator, theologian. He can seem overwhelming but there are also passages which show us about the man himself.

Cyprian, *d.* 258. Bishop of Carthage in 248 (only two years after his conversion to Christianity), he has left us many short treatises and letters from which we gain a sense of the strength of his life of prayer based on his faith in Christ.

Ephrem, *c.* 306–373. In this Syrian Father we have a glimpse of the extraordinary rich, imaginative, poetic strain of the East, for most of what he wrote was in verse and his delight in image and symbol means that as one reads him, amazing depths reveal themselves.

John of Forde, 1145–1214. A Devonshire man who entered the Cistercian abbey of Forde in his native county and became abbot in 1192. Yet another of these amazing twelfth-century Cistercians whose work repays study.

Guerric of Igny, *c.* 1070–1157. His life was lived in quiet obscurity in this Cistercian abbey near Reims but his collection of sermons which he preached on Sundays and feast days make him one of the most delightful of all the twelfth-century Cistercians.

St Gregory of Nyssa, *c.* 330–395. Called 'the father of Christian mysticism', his writing shows both his intellectual and his spiritual depths. In some of his homilies he developed a theology of the advance of the soul into the darkness of God and he thus stands near the beginning of a tradition that stretches through the medieval English mystics and St John of the Cross.

Hildegard of Bingen, 1098–1179. From 1136 she was abbess of the monastery of Rupertsberg near Bingen. She has become justly popular in recent years, for not only did she write theologically but she painted and also composed music. One of the favourite words was *viriditas*, 'greening', and she had a lively interest in the natural world and wrote on rivers, plants and animals.

Isaac of Stella, *c.* 1105/20–1178. Like Guerric he lived his life in community. From 1147 he was abbot of Stella in Poitou and then later made a new foundation near La Rochelle. His sermons show a combination of intellectual rigour with tender, human sensitivity that make him one of the particularly attractive Cistercians of his day.

St John Chrysostom, *c.* 347–407. He was known as 'the golden-mouthed'. After a period of great austerity as a hermit, he became a priest, famous for his homilies and then in 387 Patriarch of Constantinople until exile in 404 and death in 407.

Thomas Merton, 1915–1968. An American Trappist monk, who captured the imagination of thousands in his first book, his autobiography, *The Seven Storey Mountain*, and followed that with prolific writing, books, articles, poetry, letters, diaries. His achievement was to show the contemporary world that the monastic life is neither remote nor irrelevant and that living from a contemplative centre can be natural for anyone today.

St Seraphim of Sarov, 1759–1833. Called 'one of the three greatest saints of Mother Russia', he was a monk at eighteen. He became known as a Starets, or Elder of the Faith and his reputation for holiness attracted many pilgrims. He customarily addressed anyone to whom he spoke as 'My Joy'.

Symeon the New Theologian, 949–1022. He was regarded as one of the greatest of Byzantine mystical writers, who taught that union with God is a normal development of Christian life and emphasized the personal union of each Christian with Christ through the indwelling spirit.

Acknowledgements and Sources

The verses from the Psalms which appear at the beginning of each section are taken from Jim Cotter, *Through Desert Places, A Version of Psalms 1–50* (1989); *By Stony Paths, A Version of Psalms 51–100* (1991); *Towards the City, A Version of Psalms 101–150* (1993), all published by Cairns Publications.

I am most grateful to Bonnie Thurston for allowing me to include a selection of her poems. Where they have been published elsewhere, details are shown. Bonnie Thurston lives in the hills of West Virginia. Ordained, she has taught theology at university for many years and has published ten theological titles and two volumes of verse, *The Heart's Lands* and *Hints and Glimpses* (Three Peaks Press, 9 Croesonen Road, Abergavenny NP7 6AE, Wales, 2001 and 2004)

'Introvert's Insight' (Starting Point) *Hints and Glimpses* and the *Journal of Pastoral Care and Counseling* 57/2, North Carolina, 2003
'Prayer' (Silence) *Monastic Inter-Religious Dialogue Bulletin 70*, Washington DC, 2003
'Abram at Haran' (Change) *The Merton Journal* 10/1, Abergavenny, 2003
'Teacher Let Me See' (Attention)
'The Stone' (Dark and Light) *Hints and Glimpses, Pacific Church News* 141/1, 2002 and *The Merton Journal*
'A Life Not My Own' (Gift) *National Catholic Reporter* 39/32, Missouri, 2003

I am grateful to Ann Lewin for her three poems, 'Be Still' (Silence), 'Disclosure' (Mystery) and 'Jeu D'Esprit' (Epilogue)

The Basil Hume quotation (used in Starting Point) is taken from an address given to the Parliamentary Christian fellowship on 10 July 1996, printed in *The Tablet*, 12 July 1997.

The Jean Danielou quotation is taken, and then rather freely adapted, from his *The Lord of History*, London, 1958.

Ruth Bidgood, who is a neighbour in the Welsh Marches, has allowed me to include 'Roads' (Change), originally published in *The Given Time*, 1972 and reprinted in *Selected Poems*, Bridgend, Seren Books, 1992, p. 59, and 'Prayer' (Dark and Light) from *Not Without Homage*, Swansea, Christopher Davies, 1975, p. 31.

The Euros Bowen poem, 'Gloria' comes from *Euros Bowen Priest-poet*, ed. Cynthia and Saunders Davies, Penarth, Church in Wales Publications, 1993, p. 143.

Sister Monika Clare Chosh was kind enough to let me see her adaptation of a translation of St Seraphim of Sorov, which I use in 'Silence'.

I have taken two poems by John V. Taylor from his *A Christmas Sequence and Other Poems*, Oxford, The Amate Press, 1989. Permission sought.

The few sentences from Rowan Williams, which I include in 'Change', appeared in a diocesan newsletter when he was Bishop of Monmouth.

For the lines from D. Gwenallt Jones (Attention) see *Sensuous Glory. The Poetic Wisdom of D. Gwenallt Jones*, ed. Donald Allchin, D. Densil Morgan and Patrick Thomas, Norwich, Canterbury Press, 2000, p. 20.

The Edwin Muir poem is 'The Way' from *Collected Poems*, London, Faber & Faber, 1960. Permission sought.

I am grateful to an old friend, Fr Kilion McDonnell OSB of St John's, Collegeville, for allowing me to include his poem 'Perfection' in a slightly shortened form.

R S Thomas' poem 'The Bush' is taken from *Later Poems 1972–1982*, London, Macmillan, 1983. Permission sought.

The Kathleen Raine poem is 'Seventh Day' from *The Year One*, 1952, in *Selected Poems*, Golgonooza Press, 1983, p. 47. Permission sought.

Every effort has been made to trace copyright ownership of items within this book. The publisher would be grateful to be informed of any omissions.